NEW CRAFTS

MOSAICS

NEW CRAFTS
MOSAICS

HELEN BAIRD

PHOTOGRAPHY BY TIM IMRIE

LORENZ BOOKS
NEW YORK • LONDON • SYDNEY • BATH

This edition published in 1997 by
Lorenz Books, 27 West 20th Street,
New York, New York 10011

Lorenz Books are available for bulk
purchase for sales promotion and for
premium use. For details, write or call
the manager of special sales:
Lorenz Books, 27 West 20th Street,
New York, New York 10011;
(212) 807-6739

Lorenz Books is an imprint of
Anness Publishing Limited

ISBN 1 85967 382 1

Publisher: Joanna Lorenz
Senior Editor: Lindsay Porter
Designer: Lilian Lindblom
Photographer: Tim Imrie
Stylist: Fanny Ward
Illustrators: Madeleine David and
Vana Haggerty

Printed and bound in Hong Kong

Picture Credits
Thanks to e.t. archive for the photographs on pages 8, 9, 10 and 11.

1 3 5 7 9 10 8 6 4 2

CONTENTS

INTRODUCTION

To learn to make a mosaic may seem a daunting task, but in reality few things could be simpler. A mosaic can be made out of any material that can be embedded into or stuck onto another.

Traditional materials such as smalti, vitreous glass and stone are still available, but modern artists also make use of tiles, china, mirror and glass, which can be broken into regular pieces or broken haphazardly for a crazy paving effect. Materials such as beads, shells, stones, seeds, and fragments of plastic, metal and wood can all be used. Before beginning to experiment, it is useful to acquire a good basic knowledge of the techniques involved, and it is important to understand the properties of the materials you are using. As these skills are simple to acquire, in very little time you will be creating your own dazzling pieces.

Left: Almost any surface can be embellished with mosaics, from simple ceramic tiles to glass or wood — or even polystyrene.

HISTORY OF MOSAICS

THE WORD "MOSAIC" CONJURES UP IMAGES OF ROMAN FLOOR AND WALL DESIGNS, PICTURES MADE FROM SMALL, GEOMETRIC-SHAPED STONES. THIS IS ONLY PART OF THE STORY, HOWEVER, EVEN THOUGH THE WORD MOSAIC DOES HAVE ITS ORIGINS IN ITALY. AS A MEDIUM, MOSAIC CERTAINLY EXISTED LONG BEFORE THE ROMANS AND HAS BEEN USED IN MANY WAYS AND FOR VARIOUS PURPOSES BY SUBSEQUENT CULTURES AND CIVILIZATIONS UP THROUGH THE PRESENT DAY. MOSAIC HAS BEEN DEFINED AS "A SURFACE DECORATION MADE BY INLAYING SMALL PIECES OF VARYINGLY COLORED MATERIAL TO FORM A PATTERN OR PICTURE." WHILE THESE SMALL PIECES OF MATERIAL ARE USED TOGETHER TO FORM A WHOLE SURFACE PATTERN OR DESIGN, THEY RETAIN THEIR INDIVIDUAL IDENTITIES WITHIN THE MOSAIC. ALTHOUGH MOSAICS OFTEN HAVE A PURELY DECORATIVE FUNCTION, BECAUSE THE MATERIALS USED TO MAKE THEM ARE USUALLY VERY HARD-WEARING, THEY ARE OFTEN GIVEN A FUNCTIONAL ROLE AS FLOOR OR WALL COVERING AS WELL.

The earliest surviving mosaics were made in about 3000 BC by the Sumerians in ancient Mesopotamia, the area now known as Iraq. These consisted of arrangements of colored clay pegs that were pressed into wall surfaces. Later, the Egyptians used fragments of colored materials and semi-precious stones to decorate walls and to inlay furniture, decorative objects and items of jewelry.

Ancient Greece is the earliest civilization known to have used natural stones and pebbles in a variety of colors to create permanent designs, and was probably the originator of what we today think of as "mosaic." The Romans built on this technique, standardizing practices by cutting natural stone into regular cubes. They also used fired clay and a little glass for special effects. Another Roman innovation was the use of cements and mortars. These made their mosaics much more durable than those of their predecessors, and as a result there are many surviving examples of floor and wall mosaics throughout countries that were once part of the Roman Empire.

Right: A mosaic portrait of a Roman woman, dating from the 1st century AD. The colors and patterns of the mosaic pieces have been used to great effect in creating the contours of the features.

Left: Roman pavement mosaic depicting a banquet with musicians, 1st–2nd century AD.

Below: Detail from the church of San Vitale, Ravenna, 6th century AD, depicting the Emperor Justinian.

The Romans used an extraordinarily varied range of styles and subjects in their mosaics – from realistic, observed studies of everyday life to naive garden mosaics, from depictions of the gods in the received format to purely decorative designs and geometric borders.

These early mosaics were executed in the natural colors of the materials they were made from, such as grays, terracotta, ochre, black, white, muted blues and greens. The growth of Christianity introduced new subject matter, but techniques and colors remained broadly unchanged until the Byzantine era, usually dated as beginning with the reign of the Emperor Justinian in Ravenna, about AD 527. This was a very rich and innovative period in the history of mosaic, exemplified by the beautiful, luminous creations adorning Byzantine churches.

At this time, Ravenna was a wealthy imperial town and the main trading link between east and west. It is here that the best examples of Byzantine mosaic can be found, and the influence of Eastern art is apparent in the designs, such as the large Egyptian eyes, flattened shapes and ordered poses. This iconoclastic style was rendered with a new kind of tesserae – glass "smalti." Glass, which previously had been used sparingly for highlights, now became the main component of mosaics. It was fired with metallic oxides, copper and marble or had gold and silver leaf sandwiched in it. This new material gave mosaic artists access to a large palette of luminous colors. They also developed the technique of setting the pieces into the mortar bed at varying angles, thus achieving wonderful effects with the reflective qualities of glass.

When Ravenna ceased to be the main link between Europe and Asia, and its trade and wealth were taken over by Venice, the art of mosaic-making soon followed. Records show that a school of Venetian mosaicists was established as early as AD 979. The traditions of the Byzantine school were carried on there, then moved to Constantinople, the center of orthodox Christianity at the time. The art reached its peak in the 13th century.

With the dawning of the Renaissance, mosaicists became preoccupied with refining their technical abilities and, as did painters of the time, they tried to represent space, line and form. By the late 16th century, mosaic was imitating painting so completely that mosaicists were able to imitate brushstrokes, as, for example, in the huge mosaics created in St. Peter's Basilica in Rome.

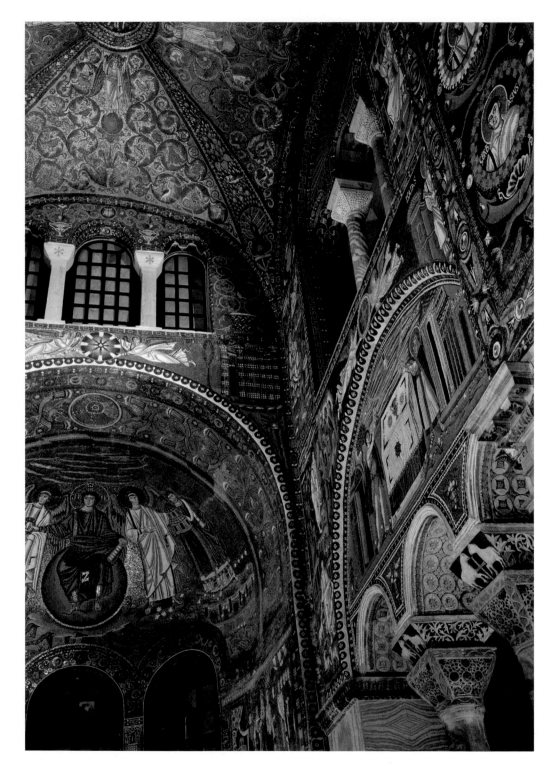

Above: Interior of San Vitale, Ravenna, showing the apse and Byzantine columns.

During this period, the art of mosaic-making was superseded by fresco painting. The mosaics that did continue to be created tended to be copies of paintings. This tendency persisted right up to the 20th century. As a result, the mosaicist had become a master craftworker and copyist rather than an original artist.

At the beginning of the 20th century, the Art Nouveau movement gave artists a new direction, and mosaic was seen as an artistic medium that could be celebrated for its own qualities. Pure pattern re-emerged and forms were simplified and stylized.

Mosaic was freed even more with the onset of modernism. The best-known exponent of mosaic in this era was the architect Antonio Gaudí (1852–1926). He covered the large exterior surfaces of his buildings, both plain and formed, with irregularly shaped colored tiles. He also commissioned prominent modern artists of the time, including Kokoschka, Klimt and Chagall, to make designs for the mosaics which clad his buildings. Examples of his mosaics include the facade of Casa Battló, the spires of the Sagrada Familia, the serpentine benches on the terrace of Güell Park and Barcelona's cathedral.

A collaborator of Gaudí, José Maria Jujal, is also worthy of mention for the ceramic medallions he made for the ceiling of the Hypostyle Hall in Güell Park. He set brilliantly colored mosaic pieces (tesserae) against ceramic fragments such as bases of bottles, cups and dishes, arranged in patterns of stars and spirals.

But the history of mosaics is not confined to western Europe. In Central America, long before the arrival of Europeans, the Aztecs and Mayas developed mosaic techniques separately from the rest of the world. There, mosaic was not used to convey images or systematic patterns, as was the tradition in Europe.

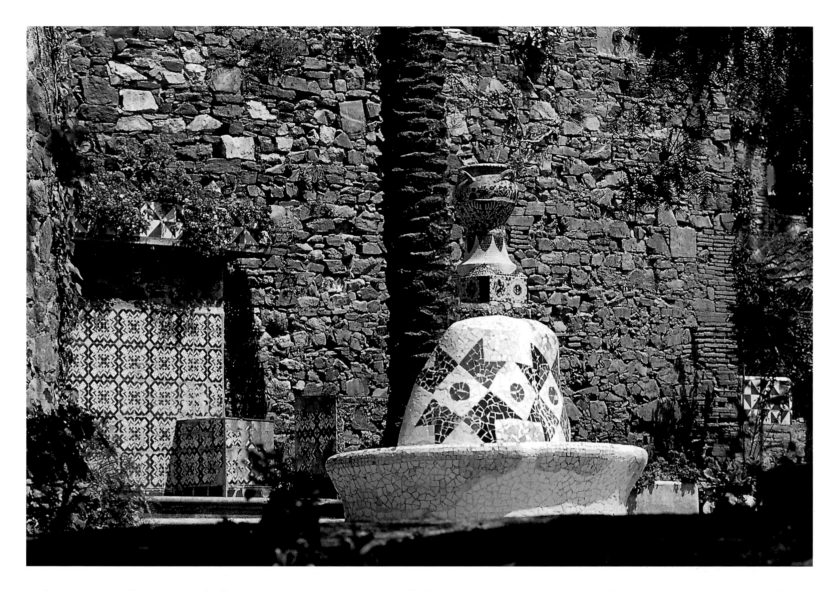

Rather, it was simply used to embellish three-dimensional forms, very beautifully, using tesserae made from fragments of precious materials, most often turquoise and coral. These objects were often of a votive or ceremonial nature, such as skulls, weapons and carved snakes, and were encrusted with a variety of precious materials to give them color, beauty and importance.

Mosaic is an important component of Islamic art. The designs are closely related to the buildings in which they are set and seem to rise naturally from the architecture. A fine example of the Islamic mosaic tradition can be seen in the 14th-century palace of the Alhambra in Granada, Spain, and Muslim craftsmen still construct complicated geometric mosaics today.

Many cultures use mosaic-like effects to adorn buildings and objects. In African art, for example, everyday objects are often studded with tacks or covered in colored beads. The effect is that of mosaic, although the method by which the pieces are attached differs.

The handwoven carpets of India and Turkey are in many ways comparable to the medium of mosaic. The patterns are made up of individual units of color and, indeed, these can be very useful as inspiration for designs. Today mosaic artists draw their inspiration from many different cultures and traditions and combine these influences with techniques and ideas that developed in Europe.

Above: Antonio Gaudí's mosaic tiles in the garden at Belleguarde, Barcelona.

GALLERY

Mosaic-making is an ancient craft with a rich history. Today, designers and craftspeople are drawn to the medium for its decorative qualities and versatility. Mosaics can be made from all manner of materials, from the traditional smalti and tesserae, to china, glass, mirrors and even plastic. These examples of contemporary work range from pieces that reflect their classical antecedents, to modern abstract designs.

Above: TEMPLE
Inspired by the embroidered decorations of Rajasthan, this piece incorporates vitreous glass and broken tiles.
NIKKI GREAVES

Above right: ADAM AND EVE
This pillar is modern in its design and materials, using a "crazy paving" effect to create the pattern set into a solid concrete base, while the theme depicted reflects the historical precedents of mosaic decoration.
HELEN BAIRD

Right: STILETTOS
These sculptures were created exclusively from pieces of mirrored glass on sculpted polystyrene bases. The sinuous, almost organic shape of the shoes is enhanced by the reflective qualities of the mirror.
REBECCA NEWNHAM

Left: ABSTRACT TABLE
The perfect combination
of old and new, resulting
in a contemporary yet
pleasingly classic piece.
The tonal range and
carefully considered sizes
of the mosaic pieces create
a harmonious design.
ZOE CANDLIN

Below: PICTURE FRAMES
The artist has made great
use of contrasting textures
in these delightful picture
frames, setting jewel-
bright glass spheres and
fragments into rough
plaster backgrounds.
LUCIANA IZZI

Right: BEFORE SCHOOL
DINNER
A wonderfully quirky
piece composed of
fragments of china set on a
wok base.
CLEO MUSSI

Right: FISH PANEL
This relatively simple design makes use of the inherent pattern-making qualities of tesserae to great effect. While the background pieces are composed in a regular grid pattern, the fish are made of fragments of tiles that suggest both scales and movement.
MOSAIC WORKSHOP

Below: EMBELLISHED CABINET
This charming cabinet is made of papier-mâché, decorated with a mosaic top. Naive designs worked in pulped paper on the sides of the cabinet echo the style of the parrot design on the top.
EMMA SPRAWSON

Left: SUNFLOWER TABLE
Broken china and discarded pottery make up this delightful table design.
NORMA VONDEE

Right: THE ALLOTMENT
Whole vitreous glass tiles
are combined with
carefully shaped pieces to
make up this charming
design. The perspective is
flattened intentionally,
creating an effect
reminiscent of early folk-
art designs.
MOSAIC WORKSHOP

Above: BIRD TABLE
Here, the mosaic pattern was inlaid into a specially built wooden table top, allowing the border of the table to become part of the design. The flowing lines and bird patterns are reminiscent of medieval tapestry designs.
ELAINE GOODWIN

Left: SILVER GILT MIRROR
For this elegant design, the natural beauty and cool colors of the materials are used to great effect.
ESTITXU GARCIA

Right: FIRE
SALAMANDER
Traditional marble tiles
were used to produce this
paving slab. Movement
and interest are created by
the positioning of the
marble tesserae in the
manner of early classical
mosaicwork.
MARTIN CHEEK

Right: GREEK TABLE
Simplicity itself, this
pleasing table design is
reminiscent of Greek
friezes.
NORMA VONDEE

MATERIALS

TESSERAE IS THE TERM GIVEN TO THE INDIVIDUAL PIECES WHICH, WHEN PUT TOGETHER, MAKE A MOSAIC. THESE CAN BE MADE FROM ALMOST ANY SOLID SUBSTANCE. FOR PRACTICAL PURPOSES, ONLY THOSE MOST COMMONLY USED ARE LISTED IN THIS BOOK. THE CHOICE OF TESSERAE DEPENDS UPON THE USES OF THE MOSAIC; FOR EXAMPLE, A HARD-WEARING MATERIAL IS NEEDED FOR A MOSAIC THAT WILL BE WALKED ON. TAKE THIS INTO ACCOUNT WHEN DECIDING ON YOUR MATERIALS.

Adhesives When choosing the correct adhesive, two considerations must be taken into account. First, should the glue be waterproof? Second, is the glue suitable for sticking the tesserae to the base? White glue is most frequently used and is excellent for securing most tesserae to a wooden base. For sticking tesserae to glass, use silicone sealant. For sticking glass to metal, use epoxy resin, which should also be used with other materials when greater strength or weather resistance is required.

Bases Mosaic can be made on top of almost any surface, as long as it is rigid and correctly pre-treated and the environment in which the mosaic is to be placed is taken into account. For example, if a mosaic is being made to stand outside, it would be unwise to secure it to a base material that may warp or expand when exposed to damp conditions. One of the most popular bases for a mosaic with a flat surface, such as a table top, is plywood (exterior-grade or marine), as it is strong and warp-resistant.

Cement mortar is often used as the base for a mosaic. It can also be used to secure the mosaic to its base as well as to grout between the tesserae. It is very easy and cheap to make: three parts builder's sand mixed with one part cement and enough water to make it pliable. Cements are also available with adhesive added to them. This gives the cement extra adhesive qualities and more flexibility. Specialty dyes can also be added to cement.

China Old plates and cups can make very interesting tesserae. Often they have patterns that can be incorporated into the design of the mosaic. However, the uneven surface they create makes them unsuitable for use in some mosaics.

Grout Mosaics are often grouted with cement; however, specialty grouts are also used. These usually have a smoother texture and can be bought in a variety of colors. They can also be colored with most water-based household and acrylic paints.

Marble comes in a wide range of colors and can be bought pre-cut into small squares. It is possible to cut marble tiles into squares yourself, but special tools are needed to do this. Marble tiles can also be broken up into irregular shapes using an ordinary household hammer. When doing this, wear protective eye covering, or cover the marble with sacking.

Mirror Add shards of broken mirror to add reflective qualities to your mosaic. Cover the mirror with sacking and break with a hammer, or use tile nippers to cut more exact shapes.

Paper This is useful as a base when creating mosaics using the semi-indirect method. (See Basic Techniques)

Plastic Although not a traditional material, interesting effects can be achieved using pieces of plastic or other man-made materials as tesserae.

Shellac This can be used to seal the finished pieces.

Smalti This is opaque glass cut into regular-shaped chunks. Made by firing glass with oxides, metals and powdered marble, it has a softly reflective surface and is available in a large variety of colors. Gold and silver smalti are made by sandwiching gold and silver leaf in transparent, colored glass.

1 Glass smalti
2 Broken mirror
3 Vitreous glass
4 Broken tiles
5 Gold-leaf smalti
6 Broken china
7 Powdered cement
8 Epoxy resin
9 Brown paper
10 Paper glue
11 Powdered tile grout
12 White glue
13 Shellac

Tiles Ceramic tiles are available in an almost unlimited range of colors and textures. Most can be cut into small pieces with tile nippers, but if not, they can usually be broken with a hammer (as with marble, protect your eyes when doing this).

Vitreous glass These mosaic pieces are manufactured glass squares, flat on one side and corrugated on the other. The color range is not quite as large as that of smalti, but they are a lot cheaper and easier to cut. Also, the material is very hard-wearing.

EQUIPMENT

MANY OF THE TOOLS NEEDED TO MAKE MOSAICS ARE VERY EASY TO FIND, AND MOST CAN BE PURCHASED AT ANY GOOD HARDWARE SHOP. HOWEVER, MOST HOUSEHOLDS ALREADY HAVE THE NECESSARY EQUIPMENT, PARTICULARLY FOR DESIGNING AND CLEANING. BEFORE INVESTING A LOT OF MONEY IN SPECIALTY EQUIPMENT, IT IS A GOOD IDEA TO CHECK YOUR CUPBOARDS. YOU MAY FIND MANY OF THE TOOLS YOU NEED LURKING IN THE BACK.

Bench vice or clamps These may be useful for cutting out the wooden base material.

Bradawl Use for punching holes in wooden base materials if they require hanging.

Brushes If applying grout in powdered form, use a soft brush to spread the powder in the spaces between the tesserae and to brush off any excess. Use a stiff-bristled brush, such as an old toothbrush or nailbrush, to clean dried grout off the finished mosaic. Fine artists' paintbrushes may be used to apply adhesive to small tile pieces.

Chalk Use to sketch onto the base.

Craft knife or scalpel When making designs using the indirect or semi-indirect method, it may be necessary to cut the background paper away from the tesserae pieces. A sharp blade will help to do this.

Dust mask It is advisable to wear a dust mask when working with powdered grout or cement, or cleaning with diluted hydrochloric acid.

Diluted hydrochloric acid This can be used to clean cement-based grout from the finished mosaic but is not strictly necessary. If using, follow proper safety procedures by protecting your eyes and hands, wearing a mask and working in a well-ventilated area, if not outdoors.

Drill A good drill with hole-boring and rebating bits may be useful for some projects, particularly if you want to add mirror hooks or other hanging devices.

Hammer Use to smash ceramic or mirror tiles into shards. Cover with a piece of sacking to prevent slivers from flying out.

Felt-tipped marker Draw your design on to the base material with a marker.

Mixing containers Old mixing bowls and buckets are useful for mixing up grout and cement.

Palette knife A palette knife or flexible kitchen knife can be used to spread cement-based adhesive onto your base.

Pencil A pencil point or sharp stick may be used to apply glue to tiny pieces of tesserae.

Protective gloves Rubber gloves should be used when cleaning with diluted hydrochloric acid, and may be used to apply grouting to tesserae. Heavy work gloves should be worn whenever you are breaking tesserae with a hammer.

Rulers and tape measures Use to measure and plan designs that require accuracy.

Sacking or old cloths Use to cover tiles before smashing with a hammer to prevent small pieces from dispersing.

Safety goggles Wear when breaking tiles with a hammer or when cleaning finished mosaics with diluted hydrochloric acid.

Sandpaper Coarse-grade sandpaper can be used to sand down the edges of wooden base materials. Fine-grade sandpaper can be used in some instances for cleaning.

Saws Different types of saw are useful for cutting your wooden base material. Use a hacksaw for basic shapes, and a jigsaw for more complicated designs.

Spatula Use a spatula for spreading glue or other smooth adhesives, such as cellulose filler, onto your base material.

Sponges and old cloths Use for wiping off excess adhesive and for polishing.

Squeegee This may be used to apply grout between tesserae, particularly if the surface of the design is very flat.

1 Jigsaw
2 Vice
3 Pencil
4 Ruler
5 Felt-tipped marker
6 Hammer
7 Right-angled ruler
8 D-clamp
9 Craft knife
10 Pliers
11 Scissors
12 Trowel
13 Spatula
14 Drill
15 Soft brush
16 Fine paintbrush
17 Tape measure
18 Grout spreader
19 Flexible knife
20 Sponge
21 Dust mask
22 Sandpaper
23 Tile nippers
24 Nailbrush
25 Bradawl
26 Safety goggles
27 Plant mister
28 Chalk
29 Masking tape

Tile nippers These are invaluable for cutting tesserae to any shape required. For shapes with rounded edges, such as circles or hearts, use to nibble away the edges, a small amount at a time, until the desired shape is achieved.

Trowel or notched cement spreader Use either of these for spreading grout and cement-based adhesive.

BASIC TECHNIQUES

Whereas EMBARKING ON YOUR FIRST MOSAIC, IT IS ADVISABLE TO USE A VERY SIMPLE DESIGN. OFTEN, THESE SIMPLE DESIGNS CAN PRODUCE THE MOST EFFECTIVE MOSAICS. CONCENTRATE ON COMBINATIONS OF THE COLORS AND TEXTURES IN THE TESSERAE YOU CHOOSE. LAY THE TESSERAE SIDE BY SIDE AND LOOK AT THE EFFECT OF THE DIFFERENT ELEMENTS. WHEN YOU ARE SURE THE COMBINATIONS WORK, YOU CAN COMMIT YOURSELF TO STICKING THE TESSERAE TO THE BASE.

CUTTING TESSERAE

1 There are three basic methods for cutting tesserae. The first and most flexible method is to use tile nippers, which are very simple to operate. Hold the material to be cut between the tips of the cutting edges of the nippers. Squeeze the handles together, and the tesserae should break in two along the line of impact. Nippers are also useful for making a specific shape.

2 When breaking up larger materials such as tiles and plates, and if regular shapes are not required, the simplest technique is to break the tesserae with a hammer. When doing this, always wear a pair of goggles or cover the tesserae with an old dish cloth.

3 The third technique is to use a special piece of equipment that consists of a small tungsten-tipped anvil, which should be embedded in a log, and a curved tungsten-tipped hammer. It is generally used for cutting smalti or marble into regular shapes. Hold the material to be cut over the anvil between your thumb and forefinger, then bring down the hammer on the material, in line with the tip of the anvil. The smalti or marble should fracture cleanly along the line of impact.

SETTING TESSERAE ON THE BASE

Direct method

This method is used for most of the projects illustrated in this book. The tesserae are simply stuck, face up, onto the base. When setting a mosaic on a three-dimensional object or an uneven surface, this method may be the only feasible way of working.

1 For the direct method, simply cover the base with a layer of cement or tile adhesive and push the tesserae into it randomly.

2 If you are following a more exact design, apply cement or tile adhesive to the individual tesserae and then stick them to the base. In this way, any design drawn on the base will not be obscured by having adhesive spread all over it.

3 If the tesserae have a reflective quality, the direct method allows them to be laid on the base at slightly different angles. This causes light to be reflected at different angles, and the mosaic will appear to shimmer.

Indirect method

Originally this technique was devised as a way of making large-scale mosaics off-site, so they could be transported ready-made, then laid in position. When using this method, the design is sectioned into manageable areas, and each area is formed into a mosaic slab, as described below. The slabs are transported to the chosen site and fitted together to form the finished mosaic.

1 Make a wooden frame to the desired proportions of the finished slab, attaching the corners with 1-inch screws. Grease the inside of the frame with petroleum jelly to help prevent the cement from sticking to the wood. Make a template of the slab by drawing around the inside of the frame on brown paper. Draw a simple design on the paper within the marked parameters, taking care to leave a 1/16-inch margin around the outer edge.

2 Cut vitreous glass tesserae to the required shape and size. Using a water-soluble adhesive, paste them face down on the brown paper, carefully following the lines of your design. Other tesserae can be used for this method, but vitreous glass has the advantage of being the same color front and back, therefore greatly reducing the likelihood of making mistakes when positioning individual pieces.

3 When the glued tesserae have dried, place the frame carefully over them, using the guidelines to make sure the frame is in exactly the right position. Sprinkle dry sand over the design and use a soft brush to nudge the sand into the crevices between the tesserae.

4 On a board, mix three parts sand with one part cement. When this is fully mixed, pile it into a mound and make a well in the middle. Pour water into the well and mix with a trowel. Continue to add water and mix until the consistency of the resulting mortar is pliable but not runny.

5 Carefully half-fill the frame with this mortar, making sure it is pressed into the corners. Cut a square of chicken-wire a little smaller than the frame, and place this on top of the cement mortar; make sure that the wire does not touch the sides of the frame. Fill the frame with the rest of the mortar. Smooth the surface with the trowel or a straight piece of wood. Place damp newspapers, then polythene sheeting over the frame and let dry for five or six days. The drying has to be as slow as possible to let the slab dry uniformly, and to avoid the possibility of cracks forming.

6 When dry, turn over the slab and its frame and dampen the brown paper with a sponge. The paper should then peel away cleanly. Loosen the screws holding the frame together and remove the slab from the frame. To finish, the face of the slab may need grouting and cleaning.

Semi-indirect or Half-and-half

This method is a combination of the direct and indirect methods described above. As with the fully indirect method, the tesserae are glued into position away from the intended site but are actually set into cement on site. This method allows mosaics to be made up easily in irregular shapes. Their light weight is especially good for attaching the mosaics to walls. Like the indirect method, this technique is useful when a smooth, flat surface is required.

1 Draw the design on brown paper and stick the tesserae face down on it, using a water-soluble glue.

2 Spread mortar over the area designated for the mosaic. A template of the mosaic can be used to mark the exact proportions. Press the tesserae into the mortar, paper side up.

3 Let dry for 24 hours; if the mosaic is situated outside, keep it from getting wet. When it is dry, dampen the paper with a wet sponge and, once the moisture has soaked through to the glue, peel away the paper, leaving the tesserae in position. The mosaic surface is now ready to be grouted and cleaned.

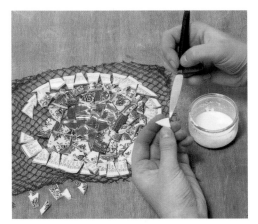

4 Another method of applying a mosaic in a semi-indirect fashion is to stick the tesserae in position on netting using a white glue, but with the tesserae placed face up.

5 When the tesserae are secure on the netting, press the mosaic, face up, into cement. Let dry before grouting and cleaning. This semi-indirect method can result in an undulating surface like that created when working with the direct method.

GROUTING

Mosaics are grouted primarily to give them extra strength and a smoother finished surface. The process has the added bonus of tying the tesserae together and making the mosaic look complete. Often, mosaics are left ungrouted. This is typical when smalti are used, as the ungrouted surface is considered more expressive.

When choosing which grout to use, consider the mosaic's location and therefore whether it will need to be waterproof and/or hard-wearing. Grouts come ready-mixed or in powder form. Usually they are applied to the mosaic ready-mixed. On flat surfaces, a squeegee can be used to spread the grout over the surface and push it between the crevices.

1 When grouting three-dimensional mosaics or uneven surfaces, it is easiest to first spread the grout over the surface with a flexible knife.

2 Then, wearing rubber gloves, rub the grout into the crevices.

3 When grouting large, flat areas, it is useful to spread the grout while it is in powder form. Use a powdered cement-based adhesive and spoon it onto the surface, then spread it with a soft brush.

4 When all the crevices are filled, spray the mosaic with water using a household plant mister. Make sure enough water is sprayed and absorbed into the cement.

You will probably need to repeat the process, as cement shrinks when wetted.

CLEANING

It is advisable to get rid of most of the excess grout while it is still wet. Most grouts can be scrubbed from the surface using a stiff-bristled brush, such as a nailbrush, and then polished off. Cement mortars and cement-based adhesives need rougher treatment, and you will probably need to use sandpaper. A quicker alternative is to dilute hydrochloric acid and paint it onto the surface to dissolve the excess cement. This process should be done outside, as the acid gives off toxic fumes. When the excess cement has fizzed away, wash off the residue of acid from the mosaic with plenty of water.

BOTTLE

THIS BOTTLE PROJECT IS IDEAL FOR BEGINNERS WHO WANT TO EXPERIMENT WITH VITREOUS GLASS. THE DESIGN IS VERY LOOSE AND REQUIRES VIRTUALLY NO DRAWING ABILITY. IT RELIES ON THE EFFECTS CREATED BY THE JUXTAPOSITION OF COLORS AND TEXTURES. RELATIVELY INEXPENSIVE BAGS OF TESSERAE IN MIXED COLORS CAN BE BOUGHT FROM SPECIALTY MOSAIC SUPPLIERS, AND IT IS A GOOD IDEA TO EXPERIMENT WITH THESE BEFORE PURCHASING LARGER QUANTITIES OF A SINGLE COLOR. DECORATING A BOTTLE LIKE THIS IS ALSO A GOOD WAY OF USING UP BITS OF TESSERAE THAT HAVE BEEN LEFT OVER FROM OTHER PROJECTS.

1 Clean the bottle, rub off the label and dry thoroughly. Dab silicone sealant onto the bottle using a pencil or pointed stick to form a simple line drawing, such as a series of swirls.

2 Cut white vitreous glass into small pieces, about ¹⁄₁₆ inch and ⅛ inch, using tile nippers.

3 Stick these cut tesserae to the lines drawn in silicone sealant, then let dry overnight.

4 Choose an assortment of colors from the vitreous glass and cut them into quarters. Some of the quarters will have to be cut across the diagonal, so they can fit snugly between the white swirls. Stick these to the bottle in a series of bands of color with silicone sealant. Let dry overnight.

5 Mix up some cement-based tile adhesive. Wearing rubber gloves, rub the cement into the surface of the bottle. Make sure all the crevices between the tesserae are filled, otherwise the tesserae are liable to pull away, as silicone sealant remains rubbery. Wipe off excess cement with a dry soft cloth and let dry overnight.

6 If necessary, sand the bottle down and polish with a soft cloth.

MATERIALS AND EQUIPMENT YOU WILL NEED
WINE BOTTLE • SILICONE SEALANT • PENCIL OR POINTED STICK •
VITREOUS GLASS MOSAIC TILES, INCLUDING WHITE • TILE NIPPERS • CEMENT-BASED TILE ADHESIVE •
MIXING CONTAINER • RUBBER GLOVES • SANDPAPER (OPTIONAL) • SOFT CLOTH

LAMP STAND

THE SIMPLE SPIRAL PATTERN USED TO CREATE THIS TALL, ELEGANT LAMP STAND FOLLOWS THE ONE THAT IS ALREADY PRESENT ON THE CARDBOARD TUBE USED AS A BASE. PIECES OF MIRROR HAVE BEEN ADDED TO CATCH THE LIGHT, AND THEY SPARKLE WHEN THE LAMP IS SWITCHED ON. THE CARDBOARD BASE IS INHERENTLY LIGHT AND THEREFORE TOO UNSTABLE TO BE USED AS A LAMP STAND ON ITS OWN, SO PLASTER HAS BEEN POURED INTO THE BOTTOM TO GIVE IT MORE WEIGHT AND A LOWER CENTER OF GRAVITY. IF PLASTER SEEMS TOO MESSY, YOU COULD USE MODELING CLAY OR SAND INSTEAD.

1 Draw twice around the circular end of the cardboard tube onto ⅛-inch plywood. Cut around these circles using a jigsaw and cut the cardboard tube to the length required. Drill a hole through the center of one of the plywood circles. Use a bradawl to make a hole in the cardboard tube ¾ inch from one end and large enough to take the electric flex.

2 Use wood glue to stick the plywood circle without the drilled hole to the end of the tube with the flex hole. Let dry overnight, then paint the cardboard tube with shellac.

3 Thread the flex through the hole in the cardboard tube and the hollow metal rod. Stand the metal rod inside the tube with the screw thread at the top. Mix some plaster of Paris with water and quickly pour it into the tube. Slip the second plywood circle over the metal rod and secure it with wood glue to the top of the cardboard tube. As soon as you have poured the plaster into the tube, you must work quickly to secure the top, as it is very important that the plaster dries with the rod in the upright position. Let dry overnight. ▶

MATERIALS AND EQUIPMENT YOU WILL NEED

PENCIL • CARDBOARD CARPET ROLL TUBE • ⅛-INCH PLYWOOD • JIGSAW • DRILL AND BIT • BRADAWL • WOOD GLUE • SHELLAC • PAINTBRUSH • LENGTH OF FLEX • HOLLOW METAL ROD WITH A SCREW THREAD, THE LENGTH OF THE FINISHED STAND • PLASTER OF PARIS • MIXING CONTAINER • TILES IN THREE COLORS • TILE NIPPERS • CEMENT-BASED TILE ADHESIVE • SPONGE • MIRROR • RUBBER GLOVES • FLEXIBLE KNIFE • SANDPAPER • SOFT CLOTH • COPPER TUBING • HACKSAW • LAMP FITTINGS • PLUG • SCREWDRIVER • LAMPSHADE

4 With a pencil, draw the design onto the tube, following the spiral lines that are already present on the cardboard tube. You can add variations and embellishments at this stage.

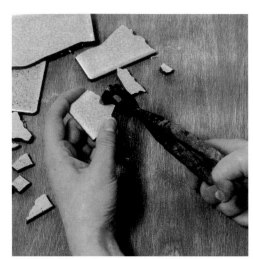

6 Select two colors of tile to fill the areas between the spiraling lines. Use the tile nippers to cut the tiles into various shapes and sizes. Cut the mirror into various shapes and sizes.

8 Wearing rubber gloves and using a flexible knife, apply wet cement-based tile adhesive over the whole area of the lamp stand, being sure to press it between all the tesserae. Wipe off the excess cement with a sponge and let dry overnight. Rub off any remaining surface cement with sandpaper, and polish with a soft cloth.

5 Cut the tiles for the outline color into small pieces using tile nippers. Stick these to the lines of your design using cement-based tile adhesive. Use a sponge to wipe away any large blobs of cement that seep out from under the tesserae, and let dry overnight.

7 Spread cement-based tile adhesive onto the remaining cardboard area, and apply the tesserae in separate bands of color. Work on a small area at a time, so the surface does not become too messy. Intersperse the colored tesserae with pieces of mirror as you work. Cover the whole cardboard tube, then let dry overnight.

9 Finish by attaching all the fittings. Slip copper tubing, cut to size, over the central rod, leaving the screw end exposed. Attach the lamp fittings, plug, and lampshade.

STORAGE CHEST

THIS SIMPLE STORE-BOUGHT CHEST WITH DRAWERS HAS BEEN TRANSFORMED BY MOSAIC MOTIFS INTO AN INDIVIDUAL, PLAYFUL PIECE OF FURNITURE. ALTHOUGH YOU MAY NOT BE ABLE TO FIND EXACTLY THE SAME CHEST, WITH A FEW MODIFICATIONS THE BASIC IDEAS CAN BE TRANSLATED TO ANOTHER PIECE OF FURNITURE. MANY WHITE TESSERAE ARE USED HERE, HELD TOGETHER WITH WHITE CEMENT, TO GIVE THE SHELF A FRESH, CLEAN LOOK THAT WOULD MAKE IT SUITABLE FOR A BATHROOM OR CHILD'S BEDROOM. WHEN TACKLING A PIECE OF FURNITURE THAT HAS MOVABLE PARTS SUCH AS DOORS AND DRAWERS, YOU NEED TO BE VERY CAREFUL THAT THE TESSERAE DO NOT IMPEDE THE MOVEMENT OF THE COMPONENTS ONCE THEY ARE APPLIED AND GROUTED.

1 Paint the shelf and drawers inside and out with watered-down white undercoat. Let dry.

2 Draw a simple motif on the front of each drawer. Choose motifs that have a bold outline and are easily recognizable when executed in one color.

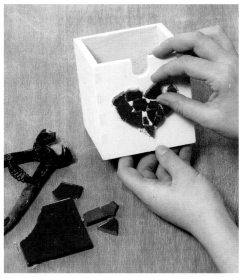

3 Cut the tiles into unevenly shaped tesserae using tile nippers. Mix up some cement-based tile adhesive, spread it within the outline of one of the motifs, then firmly press single-colored tesserae into it.

4 Surround the motif with tesserae of a different color. Be careful not to overlap the edges of the drawer. Cover the remaining drawer fronts using a different combination of two colors each time. ▶

MATERIALS AND EQUIPMENT YOU WILL NEED
STORE-BOUGHT SHELF WITH DRAWERS • WHITE UNDERCOAT • PAINTBRUSH • PENCIL • THIN TILES IN FIVE COLORS, PLUS WHITE •
TILE NIPPERS • WHITE CEMENT-BASED TILE ADHESIVE • MIXING CONTAINER • FLEXIBLE KNIFE • RUBBER GLOVES • SPONGE •
SANDPAPER • SQUARE-BOTTOMED PAINT SCRAPER

5 Cut tiny slivers of white tile. Stick these to the narrow front edges of the chest with the tile adhesive. Do this very carefully so none of the tesserae overlaps the edge.

6 Cut more white tiles into various shapes and sizes, then stick these to the large, flat outside surfaces of the shelf. When all four are covered, let the shelf and the drawers dry overnight.

7 Rub tile adhesive into the surface of the chest and drawers, wearing rubber gloves. Be especially careful when smoothing the cement into the thin edges of the shelf and the edges of the drawer fronts, making sure the cement is flush with the edges. When the gaps between the tesserae are filled, wipe off most of the excess cement with a sponge. Let the chest dry for 24 hours.

8 Sand off any remaining surface cement from the shelf and drawers. Then use an implement with a sharp, flat edge, such as a paint scraper, to scrape along the inside edge of the shelf and the sides of the drawers. Do this carefully to ensure there are no overlapping tesserae and no cement to impede the action of the drawers.

CLOCK

THIS MOSAIC CLOCKFACE IS DECORATED WITH TESSERAE MADE FROM HAND-PAINTED MEXICAN TILES IN SHADES OF BLUE, BROWN AND CREAM. PRETTY SHELLS HAVE BEEN USED HERE TO MARK THE QUARTER HOURS, ALTHOUGH THEY ARE NOT ABSOLUTELY NECESSARY. WHILE THE PAINTING ON THE TILES IS VERY FREE-STYLE AND THE TILES HAVE BEEN CUT INTO UNEVEN SHAPES, THE RESULTING TESSERAE ARE USED TO CONSTRUCT A PRECISE GEOMETRIC SHAPE. WHEN DESIGN-ING A CLOCK, YOU MUST FIRST FIND A WAY OF ACCOMMODATING THE MECHANISM THAT WORKS THE HANDS. THEN YOU MUST DESIGN THE SURFACE DECORATION TO ACCOMMODATE THE FUNCTION OF THE CLOCK. THE BASE OF THIS CLOCK IS MADE FROM TWO PIECES OF WOOD; THE THICKER PIECE AT THE BACK HAS A CIRCULAR HOLE CUT INTO IT, LARGE ENOUGH TO ACCOMMODATE THE WORKINGS AND BAT-TERIES. AS THE CLOCK MUST BE EASY TO READ, THE TESSERAE ARE LAID IN A VERY SIMPLE AND PRECISE DESIGN. IN FACT, THE PRIMARY FUNCTION OF THE DESIGN, AS WITH ANY CLOCK, IS TO DRAW ATTENTION TO THE POSITION OF THE HANDS.

1 Using a jigsaw, cut ⅛-inch plywood and ¾-inch chipboard into circles of the same diameter; the circles shown here are 16 inches in diameter. Drill a hole through the center of the chipboard circle, large enough to take the blade of the jigsaw. Saw a hole large enough to accommodate the clock's workings. Drill a hole through the center of the plywood circle, large enough to take the pivot for the clock's hands. Prime both pieces with diluted white glue and let dry.

2 Stick the plywood and chipboard circles together with strong wood glue. Clamp the pieces together with cramps; if you don't have any cramps, use weights such as heavy books. Let dry overnight.

3 Draw a circle in the center of the plywood circle. Its radius must be the length of the longest hand of the clock. Using a felt-tipped marker or pencil, sec-tion the face into quarters and use these as a basis for your design.

MATERIALS AND EQUIPMENT YOU WILL NEED

JIGSAW • ⅛-INCH PLYWOOD • ¾-INCH CHIPBOARD • DRILL AND BITS • CLOCK FITTINGS (BATTERY-OPERATED MOTOR WITH A LONG PIVOTAL PIN, AND HANDS) • WHITE GLUE • PAINTBRUSH • STRONG WOOD GLUE • CRAMPS (AT LEAST FOUR) OR HEAVY WEIGHTS • FELT-TIPPED MARKER OR PENCIL • SELECTION OF PLAIN AND PATTERNED TILES • TILE NIPPERS • CEMENT-BASED TILE ADHESIVE • MIXING CONTAINER • FLEXIBLE KNIFE • SHELLS TO MARK QUARTER HOURS (OPTIONAL) • RUBBER GLOVES • SPONGE • SANDPAPER • SOFT CLOTH

4 Cut plain tiles into small, roughly rectangular shapes using tile nippers. Mix up some cement-based tile adhesive with water and apply to the edge using a flexible knife. Press the tesserae firmly into the cement.

6 Tile the surface within the rotation area of the clock's arms, using cement-based tile adhesive applied to a small area at a time, so as not to obliterate the guidelines. Be careful to lay the tesserae flat, as they must not impede the rotation of the clock's hands.

8 Using a flexible knife, smooth cement-based tile adhesive between the tesserae around the edge of the clockface.

5 Cut patterned tiles into small irregular shapes. This design uses three kinds of patterned tiles.

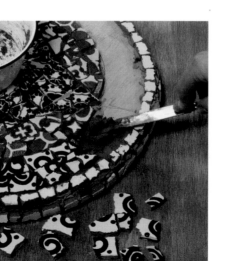

7 Tile the border, marking the positions of the quarter hours. Here, shells are used, but whatever you choose, they must not overlap the area where the hands rotate. Let dry overnight.

9 Wearing rubber gloves, rub cement-based tile adhesive over the surface of the clockface. Make sure all the gaps between the tesserae are filled, then wipe clean with a sponge. Let dry for 24 hours.

▶

10 Sand off any excess cement and polish with a soft cloth.

11 Attach the components of the clock's workings. The battery-operated workings should fit into the hole at the back. Fix the pivotal pin through the hole in the center, then fit the hands over this and secure with a nut.

POT STAND

A S WELL AS PROTECTING YOUR TABLE TOP, THIS MOSAIC POT STAND BY SARAH ROUND WILL BRIGHTEN UP ANY MEAL. THE MOSAIC IS STUCK ONTO A BOARD THAT HAS BEEN CUT INTO A GEOMETRIC SHAPE. THIS SHAPE IS INTEGRAL TO THE PATTERN IN WHICH THE TESSERAE ARE LAID. THE TESSERAE USED HERE ARE CUT CAREFULLY FROM BRIGHTLY COLORED TILES. SMALL CHIPS ARE ADDED TO PROVIDE HIGHLIGHTS TO THE AREAS OF DARKEST COLOR. BLACK TILE GROUT IS USED, BUT IF YOU CANNOT GET HOLD OF THIS, YOU COULD COLOR ORDINARY TILE GROUT WITH BLACK INK.

1 Carefully mark the proportions of the pot stand onto a square piece of chipboard; use a ruler to make sure the lines are straight.

2 Prime both sides of the chipboard with diluted white glue and let dry. Cut around the outline of the design using a jigsaw. Sand down any rough edges and prime with diluted white glue. Let dry.

3 Decide on your color scheme. Using tile nippers, cut the tiles into small pieces that will fit inside the shapes you have drawn. Here small pieces of mirror have been added to the dark blue sections of the mosaic, and small pieces of the dark blue tiles have been included in the lighter areas. Fix them in position with tile adhesive using a flexible knife. When the surface is covered, remove any excess tile adhesive with a sponge and let dry for 24 hours.

4 Fill the gaps between the tesserae with black tile grout. Rub the grout into the sides of the stand as well, then let dry for about ten minutes. Wipe off any excess grout with a sponge, then let dry for 24 hours. Paint the sides of the pot stand with diluted white glue. Cut felt to size and stick it to the back of the stand with white glue. Finish by polishing the top surface with a soft cloth and clear glass polish.

MATERIALS AND EQUIPMENT YOU WILL NEED
$\frac{1}{2}$-INCH CHIPBOARD, 12 x 12 INCHES • PENCIL • RULER • WHITE GLUE • PAINTBRUSH • JIGSAW •
SANDPAPER • TILES IN THREE COLORS • TILE NIPPERS • MIRROR • TILE ADHESIVE • MIXING CONTAINER • FLEXIBLE KNIFE •
BLACK READY-MIXED TILE GROUT • GROUT SPREADER • SPONGE • FELT • SCISSORS • SOFT CLOTH • CLEAR GLASS POLISH

COAT RACK

STORAGE OF COATS IS ALWAYS A PROBLEM, BUT IF THEY HAVE TO BE HUNG IN A HALL OR ROOM, MAKE THE RACK AN INTERESTING FEATURE RATHER THAN A NECESSARY EVIL. SANDRA HADFIELD HAS DECORATED THIS HOMEMADE RACK WITH BRIGHTLY COLORED VITREOUS GLASS TESSERAE. THESE ARE CUT INTO A VARIETY OF SHAPES AND SIZES AND ATTACHED TO THE BASE USING THE DIRECT METHOD, TO FORM BOLD OUTLINES AND BLOCKS OF COLOR. THE BASE OF THE RACK CAN BE MADE FROM MEDIUM-DENSITY FIBERBOARD OR PLYWOOD, WHICH CAN BE CUT INTO ANY SIZE AND SHAPE YOU LIKE.

1 Cut a piece of ½-inch medium density fiberboard or plywood to the length required. Draw the outline of the top on this base using a pencil and ruler to make sure the proportions are correct. Cut around the outline using a jigsaw. Sand down any rough edges.

2 Attach two mirror plates to the back of the base, one at each end. Make sure the screw holes stick out far enough from the sides of the base; when the sides are tiled with the tesserae, the holes must remain uncovered.

3 Draw the mosaic design on the surface of the base. Position the coat hooks and draw around them onto the base. ▶

MATERIALS AND EQUIPMENT YOU WILL NEED
½-INCH MEDIUM-DENSITY FIBERBOARD OR PLYWOOD • SAW • PENCIL • RULER • JIGSAW • SANDPAPER •
2 MIRROR PLATES • SCREWS • SCREWDRIVER • 3 COAT HOOKS • SHARP KNIFE • WHITE GLUE • MEDIUM AND FINE PAINTBRUSHES •
MIXING CONTAINER • VITREOUS GLASS MOSAIC TILES • TILE NIPPERS • RUBBER GLOVES • READY-MIXED TILE GROUT •
GROUT SPREADER • SPONGE • NAILBRUSH • SOFT CLOTH

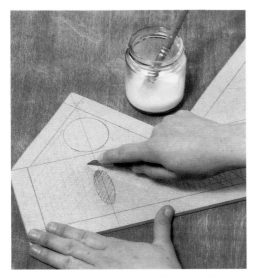

4 Score the base with a sharp knife and prime the front, back and sides with diluted white glue.

5 Here, whole blue vitreous glass tiles are alternated with half tiles around the border. Cut the tiles using tile nippers. Attach the outlining tesserae along the outside edge of the base with white glue applied with a fine paintbrush.

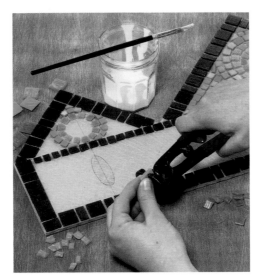

6 Stick tesserae to the areas between the main outlines. Cover the entire surface, except for the areas where the hooks will be screwed in. Cut vitreous glass tiles of the same color as the outlines in half and carefully stick them along the edges of the base. Let dry for 24 hours.

7 Wearing rubber gloves, spread grout over the surface of the mosaic, pushing it into the gaps between the tesserae. Wipe off the excess grout with a sponge and let sit for about ten minutes, so the surface dries. Then use a nailbrush to scrub off any grout that has dried on the surface of the mosaic. Let dry for 24 hours.

8 Sand off any remaining grout on the surface of the mosaic, then polish with a soft cloth. Screw the coat hooks into position, and hang in place.

HEART MIRROR

SARAH ROUND HAS DESIGNED A BOLD, PLAYFUL MOSAIC FRAME FOR THIS MIRROR, WITH A CROWN MOTIF ALONG THE TOP EDGE AND A MOSAIC HEART HANGING FROM THE BOTTOM. THE MAJORITY OF THE TESSERAE ARE MADE FROM WHITE TILES THAT HAVE BEEN INDIVIDUALLY FASHIONED TO FIT INTO ONE ANOTHER. THE HEART IS TILED WITH TESSERAE CUT FROM BLUE AND YELLOW TILES.

THESE COLORS ARE ALSO USED FOR THE SPOTS OF COLOR IN THE POINTS ALONG THE TOP OF THE MIRROR. THE USE OF BLACK GROUT GIVES A STIRRING EFFECT BY STRONGLY EMPHASIZING THE EDGES AND SHAPES OF THE WHITE TESSERAE. BLACK GROUT CAN BE DIFFICULT TO FIND, BUT YOU CAN MAKE YOUR OWN BY MIXING BLACK INK INTO WHITE GROUT POWDER.

1 Draw the outline of the frame and the position of the mirror on a piece of ½-inch chipboard. Draw the outline for the heart, which will hang from the bottom. Prime the chipboard with diluted white glue. Cut around the shapes using a handsaw or jigsaw. Sand any rough edges, then prime as before.

2 Cut three small circles from the tiles using tile nippers. To do this, cut the tiles into small squares, then nibble the corners away. Fix the circles in position along the top edge of the frame using tile adhesive. Lay the background tiles on the frame and mark the cutting lines with a washable marker.

3 Cut along the marked lines with the tile nippers.

4 Set the cut tiles in position with tile adhesive. Work around the frame, cutting and sticking the tesserae one at a time. In this way, you can cut the tesserae individually to fit neatly. ▶

MATERIALS AND EQUIPMENT YOU WILL NEED

½-INCH CHIPBOARD • MIRROR • PENCIL • RULER • WHITE GLUE • PAINTBRUSH • HANDSAW OR JIGSAW • SANDPAPER • TILES IN THREE COLORS • TILE NIPPERS • TILE ADHESIVE • WASHABLE MARKER • SPONGE • EPOXY RESIN GLUE (OPTIONAL) • BLACK READY-MIXED TILE GROUT • GROUT SPREADER • SOFT CLOTH • CLEAR GLASS POLISH • PAPER OR FELT • HANGING CLIP (D-RING) • BRADAWL • PLIERS • THICK WIRE, SUCH AS COAT-HANGER WIRE

5 Remove any excess tile adhesive from the surface or sides of the mosaic with a sponge. Place the mirror in position with white or epoxy resin glue. Let dry for 24 hours.

7 Spread grout onto the sides of the frame and heart.

9 Paint the edges of the mirror and heart with diluted white glue. Stick either paper or felt onto the back of the mirror, and attach a hanging clip. Let dry. Using a bradawl, make a hole in the middle of the bottom edge of the mirror frame and in the center of the top edge of the heart. Use pliers to cut a piece of thick wire about 2½ inches long.

6 Spread black tile grout over the surface of the frame and heart with a grout spreader, pushing it into all the gaps between the tesserae.

8 Let dry for ten minutes, then wipe off any excess grout with a sponge. Let the mirror and heart dry for 24 hours, then polish the surface with a soft dry cloth and clear glass polish.

10 Apply epoxy resin glue to both ends of the wire and to the holes made in the mirror and heart. Push the wire into these holes and let dry fully before attempting to move the mirror.

BATHROOM CABINET

IN THIS WITTY VISUAL PUN, NORMA VONDEE HAS DECORATED THE DOOR OF A BATHROOM CABINET WITH A *TROMPE L'ŒIL* MOSAIC, BEHIND WHICH CAN BE HIDDEN THE CLUTTER OF BATHROOM PILLS AND POTIONS. THE SHADOWS AND HIGHLIGHTS GIVE THE BOTTLE, GLASS AND POT THE ILLUSION OF BEING THREE-DIMENSIONAL. USE THIS PROJECT TO PRACTICE CLASSIC MOSAIC TECHNIQUES.

WHEN LAYING THE MOSAIC, PAY CLOSE ATTENTION TO THE POSITION OF EACH OF THE TESSERAE AND THE PATTERNS FORMED BY THE GAPS LEFT BETWEEN THEM. THE TESSERAE USED ARE CINCA CERAMIC MOSAIC TILES, AVAILABLE IN A WIDE RANGE OF COLORS. THEY HAVE A SOFT MATTE TEXTURE AND ARE VERY EASY TO CUT AND SHAPE, SO ARE PERFECT WHEN EXPERIMENTING WITH PRECISE MOSAICS.

1 Remove the wooden or glass panel in the door of the bathroom cabinet. Cut a ⅛-inch plywood panel to the same size. Score the surface with a sharp knife to provide a key for the white glue. Draw your design on the plywood, using the template from the back of the book. Mark in the ellipses and areas of shadow.

2 Cut the cinca mosaic tiles into precise shapes using tile nippers. Apply these

tesserae to the main outlines, fixing them in place with white glue. Be extra careful when tiling curved areas.

3 Carefully fill the areas inside the out-lines in contrasting colors. Here, reflections and highlights are depicted using different shades of tesserae to create the illusion of a three-dimensional scene. Use tesserae a shade darker than the background to tile areas of shadow.

4 Outline the shapes with a row of tesserae in the background color. If making a larger design, you could use a double row of tesserae to outline the subjects of the mosaic.

5 Fill in the background color with tesserae arranged in straight lines and let dry overnight. Secure the panel in position on the cabinet door and mask the frame with tape. Mix three parts sand and one part cement with water and a little red cement dye. Grout the mosaic with this mixture using a squeegee. Clean the surface carefully with a soft cloth and let dry as slowly as possible.

MATERIALS AND EQUIPMENT YOU WILL NEED
WALL-MOUNTED CABINET WITH DOOR • ⅛-INCH PLYWOOD • SAW • SHARP KNIFE • PENCIL •
PAPER FOR TEMPLATE (OPTIONAL) • CINCA CERAMIC TILES • TILE NIPPERS • WHITE GLUE • FINE PAINTBRUSH •
MASKING TAPE • SAND • CEMENT • RED CEMENT DYE • MIXING CONTAINER • SQUEEGEE • SOFT CLOTH

SPLASHBACK

MOSAIC IS AN IDEAL DECORATIVE SURFACE OR WALL PROTECTOR FOR AREAS IN WHICH WATER IS PRESENT, SUCH AS THIS SPLASHBACK FOR A BATHROOM SINK. IT IS MADE BY APPLYING ROUGHLY BROKEN TILES IN SUBTLE COLORS, AND CHIPS OF GLASS TO CATCH THE LIGHT, DIRECTLY ONTO A PLYWOOD BASE.

1 Measure the width of your sink and cut ⅛-inch plywood to size. Prime the surface with adhesive. When dry, draw a simple fish design on the plywood, using the template from the back of the book if required.

2 Using a bradawl, make a hole through the plywood in each corner.

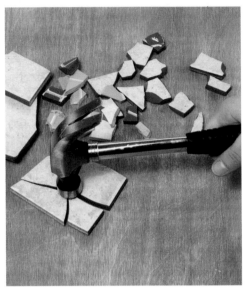

3 Select the colors of the tiles to be used for tesserae; here, two similar grays are used for the fish and a muted pink for the starfish. Wear goggles or, alternatively, cover the tiles with a cloth, then, using a hammer, smash the tiles into a variety of shapes.

MATERIALS AND EQUIPMENT YOU WILL NEED

TAPE MEASURE • ⅛-INCH PLYWOOD • SAW • WHITE GLUE • PAINTBRUSH • PENCIL • BRADAWL •
TILES IN SEVERAL COLORS • GOGGLES OR CLOTH • HAMMER • TILE NIPPERS • CEMENT-BASED TILE ADHESIVE • MIXING CONTAINER •
FLEXIBLE KNIFE • THIN EDGING TILES • MIRROR • SPOON • SOFT BRUSH • PLANT MISTER • DRINKING STRAW • SCISSORS •
SANDPAPER • SOFT CLOTH • DRILL • WALL PLUGS • 4 MIRROR SCREWS • SCREWDRIVER

4 Select a suitable tile that has a soft base with a thin glaze, such as a Mexican tile. Using the tile nippers, nibble two circles for the eyes of the fish. Then use a bradawl to carefully make a hole in the center of each.

5 Mix some tile adhesive with water and spread it onto the base within the outlines of your drawing. Set the tesserae within the drawn lines, using a lighter shade for the fins and tail and the darker shade for the body of the fish. Try to find tesserae in shapes that will fit within the drawing and suggest the movement of the fish.

6 When the fish and starfish are complete, smash tiles of the background color, in this case a soft blue. Spread cement-based tile adhesive onto the base, a small area at a time. Press the background tesserae firmly into the cement. Be careful not to tile over the holes that you have made in the corners.

7 Cut thin edging tiles into short segments and attach them around the edge of the mosaic.

8 Using tile nippers, cut the mirror into small pieces. Press these tesserae into the larger gaps in the design, on top of a blob of cement to keep them level with the other tesserae. Let dry for 24 hours.

9 Spoon dry tile adhesive onto the surface of the splashback and brush it into the cracks using a soft brush. Avoid the area around the hole in each corner. ▶

10 Spray the surface with plenty of water using a plant mister.

11 Cut a drinking straw into four pieces and stand one over each hole in the corner. Mix up some tile adhesive and grout around the straws. Let dry for 12 hours.

12 Remove the straws and sand off any cement remaining on the surface of the splashback, then polish with a soft cloth. Place the splashback against the wall and mark the positions of the screw holes. Drill the holes and insert wall plugs. Use mirror screws with metal caps to screw the splashback in position.

FIRE SCREEN

IN THIS PROJECT, MOSAIC IS USED TO DECORATE A READY-MADE FIRE SCREEN, WHICH CAN BE PURCHASED AT GOOD CRAFT STORES. ALTERNATIVELY, A SIMPLE SCREEN SHAPE CAN BE CUT FROM PLYWOOD USING A JIGSAW, AND SLOTTED INTO CUSTOM-MADE FEET. FOR HER BOLD DESIGN, SANDRA HADFIELD HAS USED VITREOUS GLASS MOSAIC TILES IN STRIKING COLORS. MOST OF THIS DESIGN USES WHOLE TILES, CUT DIAGONALLY INTO TRIANGLES.

1 Draw the design on the surface of the fire screen and its feet. Calculate the amount of space needed to accommodate the tiles required and use a ruler to mark the main areas. Score the surface with a sharp knife, then prime with diluted white glue and let dry.

2 Select vitreous glass tiles in the colors you require. Cut some tiles into triangles for the border.

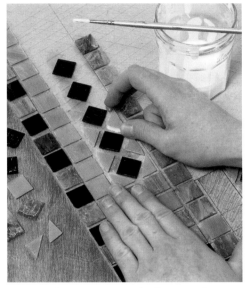

3 Fix the tesserae to the base with white glue. Try to make all of the gaps between the tesserae equal and leave the area that will be slotted into the feet untiled.

4 Tile the edge, then the feet, making sure they will still slot on to the screen. Let dry overnight. Wearing rubber gloves, rub grout into the surface of the mosaic, making sure all the gaps between the tesserae are filled. Let dry for about ten minutes, then remove any excess grout with a nailbrush. Allow the grout to dry for 12 more hours, then paint the back of the screen with wood primer, undercoat and finally gloss paint, allowing each coat to dry before applying the next. Polish the mosaic with a soft cloth and slot on the feet.

MATERIALS AND EQUIPMENT YOU WILL NEED
READY-MADE FIRE SCREEN BASE • PENCIL • RULER • SHARP KNIFE • WHITE GLUE • PAINTBRUSHES •
VITREOUS GLASS MOSAIC TILES • TILE NIPPERS • RUBBER GLOVES • READY-MIXED TILE GROUT • NAILBRUSH • WOOD PRIMER •
WHITE UNDERCOAT • GLOSS PAINT • SOFT CLOTH

LOVE LETTER RACK

PERSONAL LETTERS AND CORRESPONDENCE OFTEN HAVE A TENDENCY TO BE MISPLACED OR LOST IN A BUSY HOUSEHOLD. TESSA BROWN'S SIMPLE BUT EFFECTIVE DESIGN FOR A LETTER RACK COULD BE THE ANSWER TO THIS PERENNIAL PROBLEM. SHE HAS USED HEART MOTIFS, BUT ANY SIMPLE PATTERNS OR SHAPES COULD BE SUBSTITUTED. THE RACK IS A SIMPLE CONSTRUCTION. PIECES OF MEDIUM-DENSITY FIBERBOARD ARE CUT TO SHAPE USING A JIGSAW OR COPING SAW. THE FRONT IS DECORATED WITH VITREOUS GLASS TESSERAE, WHICH HAVE BEEN CUT CAREFULLY TO FIT THE DESIGN.

1 Draw the shapes of the components of the rack on to both pieces of fiberboard or plywood. Cut them out with a jigsaw. Prime the surfaces with diluted white glue. When dry, draw the pattern onto the front panel. Stick the pieces together with wood glue and secure with panel pins. Let dry overnight.

2 Select two tones of red vitreous glass tesserae to tile the heart motifs. Using tile nippers, nibble the tesserae

into precise shapes to fit your design. Attach in position with cellulose filler.

3 Select the colors of vitreous glass to tile around the hearts. Trim the tesserae to fit snugly around the motif and within the edges of the rack. Fix them to the base. Leave to dry overnight.

4 Smooth cellulose filler over the surface of the mosaic.

5 Rub the filler into all the gaps with your fingers. Rub off any excess filler with a damp sponge and let dry. Use sandpaper to remove any filler that has dried on the surface of the mosaic and to neaten the edges.

6 Paint the parts of the rack that are not covered with mosaic with red paint. Let dry.

MATERIALS AND EQUIPMENT YOU WILL NEED
⅛-INCH AND ½-INCH MEDIUM-DENSITY FIBERBOARD OR PLYWOOD • PENCIL • JIGSAW • WHITE GLUE • PAINTBRUSHES • WOOD GLUE • PANEL PINS • PIN HAMMER • VITREOUS GLASS MOSAIC TILES • TILE NIPPERS • WHITE CELLULOSE FILLER • GROUT SPREADER OR FLEXIBLE KNIFE • SPONGE • SANDPAPER • RED PAINT

MIRROR

MOSAIC IS A VERY EFFECTIVE WAY OF SURROUNDING A MIRROR. THE UNDU-LATING, FRACTURED SURFACE CREATED BY THE TESSERAE PERFECTLY SETS OFF THE SMOOTH, REFLECTIVE PLANE OF THE GLASS. THIS MIRROR, DESIGNED BY

CLEO MUSSI, HAS AN ATTRACTIVE FRAME TO ADD INTEREST AND ATMOSPHERE TO A BATHROOM. SHE HAS CHOSEN TO USE CHINA WITH DELICATE PATTERNS IN COOL, FRESH COLORS AND WITH TOUCHES OF GOLD.

1 Draw the outer shape of the mirror frame onto a piece of ¾-inch plywood. Cut around this shape using a jigsaw, then sand down the rough edges. Onto this base panel, draw the desired shape of the mirror glass. Here, the shape of the mirror glass echoes the shape of the panel, but it could be a completely different shape if desired. Make sure it is a shape that glass-cutters will be able to reproduce.

2 Seal the sides and front of the base panel with diluted white glue and paint the back first with wood primer, then undercoat and finally gloss paint. Mark the position of the mirror plate on the back of the panel. Using an appropriate bit, rebate the area that will be under the keyhole-shaped opening (large enough to take a screw head). Then screw the mirror plate in position.

3 Make a cardboard template in the exact dimensions of the mirror shape you have drawn on the base. Ask your supplier to cut a piece of ⅛-inch foil-backed mirror using your template.

4 Stick the mirror in position using ready-mixed tile adhesive. Let dry overnight. ▶

MATERIALS AND EQUIPMENT YOU WILL NEED

¾-INCH PLYWOOD • PENCIL • RULER • JIGSAW • SANDPAPER • WHITE GLUE • PAINTBRUSHES • WOOD PRIMER • WHITE UNDERCOAT • GLOSS PAINT • DRILL WITH REBATING BIT • MIRROR PLATE • ¾-INCH SCREWS • SCREWDRIVER • THICK CARDBOARD • ⅛-INCH FOIL-BACKED MIRROR • TILE ADHESIVE • FLEXIBLE KNIFE • MASKING TAPE • TRACING PAPER (OPTIONAL) • TILE NIPPERS • SELECTION OF CHINA • POWDERED TILE GROUT • VINYL MATTE LATEX OR ACRYLIC PAINT (OPTIONAL) • MIXING CONTAINER • GROUT SPREADER OR RUBBER GLOVES • NAILBRUSH • SOFT CLOTH

5 Trim 1/16 inch from the template all around the edge and cover the mirror with it, securing it in place with masking tape; this should prevent the mirror from being scratched. The mosaic will eventually overlap the 1/16 inches of uncovered mirror.

6 Draw the design for the frame on the dry, sealed surface surrounding the mirror; use tracing paper and a soft pencil to copy and transfer your original plan, if desired.

7 Using tile nippers, snip the smooth edges from the cups and plates you have collected. Use these to tile the outside edge of the base panel and to overlap the 1/16-inch edges of the mirror, sticking them down with ready-mixed tile adhesive. Cut the remainder of the china into small pieces and stick them to the structural lines of your design.

8 Fill in the areas of detail between the outlining tesserae. When the mirror frame is completely tiled, let it dry for 24 hours.

9 Mix powdered tile grout with water and, if desired, color with vinyl matte latex or acrylic paint. Spread this over the surface of the tesserae using a grout spreader, or wear rubber gloves and rub it in by hand, making sure all the gaps between the tesserae have been filled. Let the surface dry for a few minutes, then brush off the excess grout with a stiff-bristled nailbrush. Wipe clean with a soft cloth.

10 Let the mirror dry thoroughly overnight, then remove the protective cardboard from the mirrored glass and hang in position.

SKIRTING BOARD

A SKIRTING BOARD IS AN UNUSUAL AND DISCREET WAY OF INTRODUCING MOSAIC INTO YOUR HOME. YOU CAN USE A REPEATED ABSTRACT DESIGN, A SUCCESSION OF MOTIFS, OR A COMBINATION OF THE TWO. HERE, THE MOTIF OF A DAISY HAS BEEN REPEATED AT REGULAR INTERVALS. THE TESSERAE ARE MADE FROM MARBLE TILES THAT HAVE BEEN ROUGHLY BROKEN WITH A HAMMER. YOU WILL NEED A LARGE QUANTITY OF TILES, SO IT IS BEST TO DECORATE A SMALL ROOM.

1 Measure the room and buy lengths of skirting board to fit. Roughen the surface with coarse-grade sandpaper, then prime with diluted white glue. Let dry.

2 Mark the skirting board into small, equally spaced sections. Using a dark pencil, draw a simple motif in each section. Here, the motif is a daisy.

4 Mix up some cement-based tile adhesive and, working on a small area at a time, spread it along the lines of your drawing. Press the broken pieces of marble firmly into the cement. Choose tesserae in shapes that echo those of the design,—for example, the petal shapes of the flower. The marble can be roughly shaped by tapping the edges of larger tesserae with a hammer. When each motif is tiled, wipe off any excess cement with a sponge and let dry overnight. ▶

3 Wear goggles or cover the tiles with a cloth. Smash the marble tiles into small pieces with a hammer.

MATERIALS AND EQUIPMENT YOU WILL NEED
RULER OR TAPE MEASURE • SKIRTING BOARD • COARSE-GRADE SANDPAPER • WHITE GLUE • PAINTBRUSH •
PENCIL • GOGGLES OR CLOTH • SELECTION OF MARBLE TILES • HAMMER • CEMENT-BASED TILE ADHESIVE • MIXING CONTAINER •
FLEXIBLE KNIFE • SPONGE • RUBBER GLOVES OR SQUEEGEE • SANDPAPER • SOFT CLOTH

5 Break up tiles in the background color with a hammer. Working on a small area at a time, spread cement-based adhesive onto the untiled sections of skirting board and press the tesserae into it. When the surface is covered, use small pieces of the background color to tile along the top edge of the skirting, ensuring that the tesserae do not overlap the edge. Let dry for 24 hours.

7 Sand off any cement that has dried on the surface of the mosaic and polish the surface with a soft cloth. Set the skirting board in position.

6 Wearing rubber gloves or using a squeegee, rub wet cement-based adhesive into the surface of the mosaic, filling all the gaps between the tesserae. Use a flexible knife to spread the cement into the edge. Wipe off any excess with a cloth and let dry overnight.

AZTEC BOX

THE AZTECS AND MAYAS OF PRE-COLOMBIAN CENTRAL AMERICA USED TO DECORATE SKULLS, WEAPONS AND SNAKE SHAPES WITH PRECIOUS MATERIALS SUCH AS TURQUOISE, CORAL AND JADE. THIS DECORATION WAS INTENDED TO SEAL IN THE MAGICAL ENERGIES OF THE OBJECT AND WARD OFF EVIL. NORMA VONDEE WAS INSPIRED BY SUCH TREASURES TO MAKE THIS MOSAIC JEWELRY BOX. FOR THE TESSERAE SHE HAS USED VITREOUS GLASS AND CINCA TILES IN COLORS THAT ECHO THOSE USED BY THE CENTRAL AMERICAN ARTISTS. SHE HAS ALSO INCLUDED GLASS GLOBULES BACKED WITH GOLD AND SILVER LEAF.

1 Draw the design on the wooden box with a marker or dark pencil. Here, the teeth and jaws of the beast are drawn immediately below the opening edge of the lid.

2 Stick on glass globules for the eyes, holding them in place with masking tape until dry. Cut vitreous glass tiles in coral and stick onto the nose and lips. Cut vitreous glass tiles in pink and terra-cotta to line the lips. Use a paintbrush to apply glue to small pieces.

3 Cut black and white tesserae into precise shapes to fit the areas marked for the teeth, then stick them in position.

4 Select tesserae in varying shades of turquoise, blue and green, and use them to tile around the eye sockets and to delineate the snout, cutting them where necessary to fit the sides of the box. Include a few small glass globules positioned randomly. When tiling around the hinges, leave about ½ inch untiled, so the box can be opened easily. Let dry, then tile the lid in the same way.

5 Mix three parts sand with one part cement and add a little black cement dye. Add water a little at a time until the desired consistency is attained. Wearing rubber gloves, rub the cement onto the surface of the box. Scrape off the excess cement with a squeegee, then rub the box with a slightly damp sponge. Finish by polishing with a dry cloth, then cover the box with a plastic bag so it will dry as slowly as possible.

MATERIALS AND EQUIPMENT YOU WILL NEED

WOODEN BOX WITH HINGED LID • MARKER OR DARK PENCIL • GLASS GLOBULES BACKED WITH GOLD AND SILVER LEAF • WHITE GLUE • MASKING TAPE • MIXING CONTAINERS • FINE PAINTBRUSH • VITREOUS GLASS MOSAIC TILES • TILE NIPPERS • CINCA CERAMIC TILES • SAND • CEMENT • BLACK CEMENT DYE • RUBBER GLOVES • SQUEEGEE • SPONGE • SOFT CLOTH • PLASTIC BAG

GARDEN TABLE

THE BOLD DESIGN OF THIS TABLE TOP AND THE SIMPLICITY AND DELICACY OF THE METAL FRAME THAT SUPPORTS IT COMBINE TO CREATE A TABLE THAT WOULD LOOK GOOD IN THE CONSERVATORY, OR AS AN OCCASIONAL TABLE FOR A GARDEN OR PATIO ON A SUNNY DAY. THE TOP IS DECORATED WITH TESSERAE MADE FROM ROUGHLY BROKEN FLOOR TILES, WHICH HAVE A STRONG TEXTURE.

HIGHLIGHTS ARE CREATED BY THE INCLUSION OF TINY CHIPS OF GOLD-LEAF SMALTI. THE METAL FRAME USED HERE WAS MADE TO ORDER BY A LOCAL BLACK-SMITH, AND THERE ARE MANY SUCH CRAFTSPEOPLE WILLING TO MAKE UNIQUE PIECES OF THIS KIND. ALTERNATIVELY, FRAMES CAN OFTEN BE FOUND AT SECOND-HAND FURNITURE SHOPS.

1 Draw the shape of the table top on a piece of ¾-inch plywood. Cut this out using a jigsaw and sand off any rough edges. Then prime with diluted white glue, paying special attention to the edges.

2 Draw a simple design on the table top. You may need to use a tape measure to get the proportions right, but don't be too rigid about the geometry, as a freehand approach suits this method of working.

3 Cut floor tiles in your outlining color into small pieces using tile nippers. Try to cut them into a variety of shapes; uniform shapes would jar with the crazy paving effect of the smashed tesserae used for the rest of the table.

MATERIALS AND EQUIPMENT YOU WILL NEED

¾-INCH PLYWOOD • PENCIL • JIGSAW • SANDPAPER • WHITE GLUE • PAINTBRUSH • TAPE MEASURE (OPTIONAL) •
SELECTION OF FLOOR TILES • TILE NIPPERS • CEMENT-BASED TILE ADHESIVE • MIXING CONTAINERS • FLEXIBLE KNIFE • SPONGE •
GOGGLES OR CLOTH • HAMMER • GOLD-LEAF TESSERAE • SPOON • SOFT BRUSH • PLANT MISTER • DILUTED HYDROCHLORIC ACID (OPTIONAL) •
RUBBER GLOVES (OPTIONAL) • METAL TABLE FRAME • SCREWS • SCREWDRIVER • SOFT CLOTH

4 Mix up some cement-based tile adhesive and, using a flexible knife, spread it around the edge of the table top. Firmly press the outlining tesserae into the cement, making sure they do not overlap the edges.

6 Wear goggles or cover the tiles with a cloth. Using a hammer, smash the tiles that are to fill in the areas between the outlines.

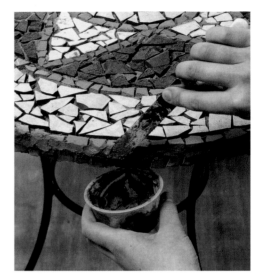

8 Using a flexible knife, smooth cement-based tile adhesive on to the edges of the table.

5 Apply the cement-based tile adhesive to the lines of your drawing and press in the outlining tesserae. Use a sponge to wipe away any large bits of cement that have squashed out from under the edges of the tesserae and let dry overnight.

7 Apply cement-based tile adhesive to small areas of the table top at a time and press in the tile fragments. Do this carefully as the finished surface needs to be as flat as possible. Let dry overnight.

9 Cut gold-leaf tesserae into tiny, irregular shapes using tile nippers. Place these in the larger gaps between the broken tiles on the table top. If necessary, first insert a blob of cement adhesive to ensure that the gold is at the same level as the tiles. Let dry overnight. ▶

10 Spoon dry cement-based adhesive onto the surface of the table. Smooth it over the surface with a soft brush, making sure all the gaps between the tesserae have been filled. Spray water over the table using a plant mister. When the cement has absorbed enough water, wipe away any excess with a cloth. If the cement sinks when wet, repeat the whole process. Let dry for 24 hours. Turn the table top over and rub wet cement-based tile adhesive into the plywood on the underside. Let dry overnight.

11 Clean off any excess cement with sandpaper. Alternatively, diluted hydrochloric acid can be used, but you must wear goggles and rubber gloves and apply it outside or where there is good ventilation. Wash any acid residue from the surface.

12 When clean, turn the table top face down and screw the metal frame in place using screws that are no longer than the thickness of the plywood. Polish the table top with a soft cloth.

FLOWERPOT

F OR THIS FLOWERPOT, COMBINING BOTH THE FUNCTIONAL AND DECORATIVE QUALITIES OF MOSAICS, CLEO MUSSI HAS CHOSEN A DESIGN AND COLORS THAT REFLECT THE FLOWERS TO BE PLANTED IN IT. SMALL SQUARES OF MIRROR ARE INCLUDED IN THE DESIGN, AS THEY WILL REFLECT THE DAPPLED LIGHT OF A LEAFY GARDEN OR CONSERVATORY. AS ONLY PART OF THE POT IS TO BE COVERED WITH MOSAIC, A READY-GLAZED, HIGH-FIRED TERRA-COTTA POT IS USED. THIS IS ESPECIALLY IMPORTANT IF THE POT IS TO BE LEFT OUTSIDE ALL YEAR. ALTERNATIVELY, IF THE WHOLE OUTER SURFACE OF A POT IS TO BE COVERED IN MOSAIC, A FROST-RESISTANT TERRA-COTTA POT MAY BE USED, AS LONG AS THE POT IS WATERPROOFED ON THE INSIDE BY SEALING IT WITH WHITE GLUE.

1 Draw a simple design on the pot, using chalk or a wax crayon.

2 Cut appropriate shapes from the china using tile nippers. Mix up some cement-based tile adhesive and use it to attach the tesserae to the pot with a flexible knife. Work first on the main lines and detailed areas, applying the adhesive to small areas at a time so you can follow the lines of the design.

3 Fill in the larger areas of plain color. When complete, let the pot dry for 24 hours.

4 Mix powdered grout with water and a little cement dye. Wearing rubber gloves, spread the grout over the pot, filling all the cracks between the tesserae. Let the surface dry, then brush off any excess grout with a nailbrush. Let the pot dry for at least 48 hours before polishing with a dry soft cloth.

MATERIALS AND EQUIPMENT YOU WILL NEED

FLOWERPOT • CHALK OR WAX CRAYON • SELECTION OF CHINA • TILE NIPPERS • CEMENT-BASED TILE ADHESIVE • MIXING CONTAINER • FLEXIBLE KNIFE • POWDERED WATERPROOF TILE GROUT • CEMENT DYE • RUBBER GLOVES • NAILBRUSH • SOFT CLOTH

DECORATIVE SPHERES

CLEO MUSSI WAS INSPIRED BY MILLEFIORI AFRICAN BEADWORK TO MAKE THESE MOSAIC SPHERES. USE THEM AS UNUSUAL GARDEN DECORATIONS, OR FILL A BOWL WITH THEM FOR A STRIKING TABLE CENTERPIECE. YOU COULD SELECT FRAGMENTS OF CHINA IN COLORS THAT REFLECT THE SEASON—FOR EXAMPLE, CITRUS COLORS FOR A FRESH SPRING FEEL; MEDITERRANEAN BLUES, WHITE AND TERRA-COTTA FOR SUMMER, GOLDS, RUSTS AND RICH BERRY COLORS FOR AUTUMN, WHITE, GRAYS AND BLACK WITH LOTS OF MIRROR FOR THE WINTER MONTHS. THE BASES USED FOR THESE SPHERES CAN BE WOOD OR POLYSTYRENE. IF POLYSTYRENE IS USED, THE SPHERES REMAIN VERY LIGHT AND WOULD MAKE EFFECTIVE HANGING DECORATIONS, SUCH AS CHRISTMAS TREE BAUBLES OR MOBILES.

1 Seal the polystyrene or wooden spheres with diluted white glue. Let dry.

2 Roughly draw a simple design onto a sphere using a pencil. A combination of circular motifs and stripes works well, but you can experiment with other geometric shapes and abstract designs.

3 Cut your china and mirror into pieces, using tile nippers; combine different sizes of tesserae. Stick the pieces to the sphere with a waterproof tile adhesive. Let dry overnight.

4 Mix grout with water and a little colored vinyl matte latex or acrylic paint. Wearing rubber gloves, rub the grout into the surface of the sphere, filling all the cracks between the tesserae.

5 Leave for a few minutes until the surface has dried, then brush off any excess grout using a stiff nailbrush.

6 Let dry overnight, then polish with a dry soft cloth. Let the spheres air for a few days before arranging.

MATERIALS AND EQUIPMENT YOU WILL NEED
10 POLYSTYRENE OR WOODEN SPHERES • WHITE GLUE • PAINTBRUSH • PENCIL •
SELECTION OF CHINA • MIRROR • TILE NIPPERS • TILE ADHESIVE • POWDERED TILE GROUT • MIXING CONTAINER •
VINYL MATTE LATEX OR ACRYLIC PAINT • RUBBER GLOVES • NAILBRUSH • SOFT CLOTH

CHINA TILES

IF YOU WOULD LIKE TO INTRODUCE MOSAIC TO AN OUTDOOR SETTING BUT ARE DAUNTED BY A LARGE PROJECT, THESE UNIQUE TILES BY CLEO MUSSI ARE THE PERFECT SOLUTION. THEY COULD BE ATTACHED TO A WALL AS AN INTERESTING FEATURE OR DISPLAYED ALONGSIDE OTHER GARDEN DECORATIONS. YOU COULD STICK A FEW TILES TO YOUR WALL, EACH IN A DIFFERENT COLOR OR DESIGN, OR REPEAT THE SAME PATTERN AT REGULAR INTERVALS. THE TILES CAN ALSO BE USED AS TABLE MATS OR COASTERS. THIS IS A GOOD PROJECT TO CHOOSE FOR YOUR FIRST ATTEMPT AT USING CHINA AS TESSERAE. DON'T BE TOO EXACTING WITH YOUR INITIAL ATTEMPTS; RATHER, THINK OF THEM AS SKETCHES OR EXPERIMENTS BEFORE EMBARKING UPON LARGER, MORE COMPLEX MOSAICS.

1 Prime the back of a plain tile with diluted white glue and let dry. Draw a simple, rough design on the back of the tile using a pencil.

2 Cut a selection of china into small pieces that will fit into your design, using tile nippers. Arrange these tesserae in groups according to color and shape.

3 Dip the tesserae into tile adhesive and press them, one by one, onto the tile, using the drawing as a guide. Make sure there is enough adhesive on the tesserae; when you press them onto the tile, glue should ooze out around the tesserae. When the tile is covered with mosaic, let dry overnight.

4 Mix acrylic paint or cement dye with powdered waterproof tile grout. Add water and mix to a dough-like consistency. Wearing rubber gloves, rub the grout into the surface of the mosaic, making sure all the gaps between the tesserae are filled. Let dry for about ten minutes.

5 Scrub the surface of the tile with a stiff nailbrush to remove all the excess grout, which should come away as powder. When clean, let the tile dry for 24 hours. Finish the tile by polishing it with a soft cloth.

MATERIALS AND EQUIPMENT YOU WILL NEED
PLAIN WHITE TILES • WHITE GLUE • PAINTBRUSH • PENCIL • SELECTION OF CHINA • TILE NIPPERS •
TILE ADHESIVE • MIXING CONTAINER • ACRYLIC PAINT OR CEMENT DYE • POWDERED WATERPROOF TILE GROUT •
RUBBER GLOVES • NAILBRUSH • SOFT CLOTH

JAM JAR NIGHT-LIGHT

HEN LIT WITH A SMALL CANDLE, THIS STAINED GLASS NIGHT-LIGHT, DESIGNED BY TESSA BROWN, THROWS PATCHES OF COLORED LIGHT ACROSS A ROOM. ONE JAR IS USED AS THE BASE AND ANOTHER IS BROKEN INTO FRAGMENTS THAT ARE PAINTED A VARIETY OF COLORS WITH STAINED-GLASS PAINTS. THESE FRAGMENTS ARE THEN STUCK ONTO THE BASE JAR AND THE GAPS BETWEEN THE GLASS ARE GROUTED. IDEALLY YOU SHOULD SELECT TWO JARS OF THE SAME SIZE, BUT IF YOU CANNOT FIND TWO EXACTLY THE SAME, USE THE SMALLER ONE AS THE BASE.

1 Wrap one of the jars in an old dish cloth. Wearing goggles and protective gloves, and covering your hair, smash the jar with a hammer. If the jars are of different sizes, smash the larger one.

3 Use reusable adhesive to pick up the broken pieces of glass and turn them over so that the sharp edges face upwards. Paint the concave surface of each fragment with stained glass paint. Here, three colors are used. Let the pieces dry.

5 Spread cellulose filler over the surface, making sure all the gaps are filled. Smooth into the top and bottom edges of the jar and wipe off most of the excess. Let dry. If the filler has settled and cracks have appeared, use more filler.

2 Pick pieces to use as tesserae. Place them on scrap paper with the sharp edges facing downwards to avoid cutting yourself. Wrap any unused glass in newspaper and dispose of it carefully.

4 Glue the painted glass fragments to the base jar, using a transparent rapid-setting epoxy resin, which must be solvent-free. Let dry thoroughly.

6 When dry, clean any excess filler with a scour pad and water. Use sandpaper to neaten the top and bottom edges. Color the filler with acrylic paint.

MATERIALS AND EQUIPMENT YOU WILL NEED
2 JAM JARS • OLD DISH CLOTH • GOGGLES • PROTECTIVE GLOVES • HAMMER • SCRAP PAPER • NEWSPAPER •
. REUSABLE ADHESIVE • STAINED-GLASS PAINTS • PAINTBRUSHES • SOLVENT-FREE, RAPID-SETTING TRANSPARENT EPOXY RESIN •
WHITE CELLULOSE FILLER • GROUT SPREADER • SCOUR PAD • SANDPAPER • ACRYLIC PAINT

STAR WALL MOTIFS

THESE LITTLE WALL MOTIFS HAVE BEEN CREATED BY CLEO MUSSI TO ADD SPARKLING FOCAL POINTS TO A GARDEN. THEY ARE PARTICULARLY EFFECTIVE WHEN DISPLAYED IN CLUSTERS OR SURROUNDED BY LUSH FOLIAGE. USING TESSERAE CUT FROM CHINA AND GLASS, THEY CAN BE MADE IN ANY SHAPE, SIZE OR DESIGN AND IN AS MANY QUANTITIES AS YOU WISH. THESE STAR MOSAICS HAVE BEEN STUCK ONTO THIN PLYWOOD BASES SO THEY CAN BE MOVABLE FEATURES. HOWEVER, IF DESIRED, THEY CAN BE MADE PERMANENT SIMPLY BY STICKING THE TESSERAE DIRECTLY ONTO THE WALL SURFACE.

1 Draw a star motif on ⅛-inch plywood using a pencil and a set square, ruler and compass.

3 Make two small holes through the star using a bradawl.

5 Cut a short length of wire and bend it into a loop for hanging the star. Push the ends through the holes in the star from the painted side and secure them to the front with staples or tape. ▶

2 Cut out the star using a coping saw or an electric scroll saw. Sand down any rough edges, then seal one side with diluted white glue.

4 Paint the unsealed side with wood primer, then undercoat and finish with a coat of gloss or matte paint. Let each coat dry before applying the next.

MATERIALS AND EQUIPMENT YOU WILL NEED
⅛-INCH PLYWOOD • PENCIL • SET SQUARE • RULER • COMPASS • COPING SAW OR ELECTRIC SCROLL SAW •
SANDPAPER • WHITE GLUE • PAINTBRUSHES • BRADAWL • WOOD PRIMER • WHITE UNDERCOAT • GLOSS OR MATTE PAINT • WIRE CUTTERS •
WIRE • STAPLER OR TAPE • SELECTION OF CHINA • MIRROR • TILE NIPPERS • TILE ADHESIVE •
POWDERED TILE GROUT • CEMENT DYE • MIXING CONTAINERS • RUBBER GLOVES • NAILBRUSH • SOFT CLOTH

6 Snip the china and mirror into small pieces using tile nippers and arrange these into groups according to color and shape.

7 Stick the china and mirror fragments to the surface of the star, one piece at a time. Take each fragment and dip it into ready-mixed tile adhesive, making sure enough is on the fragment to ooze a little from under the edges when pressed onto the base. Cover the surface of the star and let dry overnight.

8 Mix the desired quantity of grout with cement dye. Adding a little water at a time, mix until the grout is of dough-like consistency. Wearing rubber gloves, push the grout into all the gaps between the tesserae. Let dry for a few minutes.

9 Using a nailbrush, gently remove all the excess grout. This should brush away as powder; if it does not, the grout is still too damp, so let it dry for a few more minutes before brushing again.

10 Polish the surface with a soft, dry cloth, then let dry for 24 hours before hanging outside.

PRINCESS WALL MOSAIC

G ARDENS OFFER THE MOSAIC ARTIST THE OPPORTUNITY TO EXPERIMENT WITH MORE PLAYFUL WALL MOSAICS. THERE IS LESS PRESSURE TO BE "TASTEFUL," AS THE PIECES CAN BE SOFTENED BY PLANTS AND GARDEN BRIC-A-BRAC. THIS RATHER TONGUE-IN-CHEEK PRINCESS DESIGN IS APPLIED TO A WALL USING THE SEMI-INDIRECT METHOD. THIS MEANS THAT IT CAN BE MADE UP IN THE COMFORT OF YOUR HOME OR STUDIO, THEN MOVED LATER, AS A WHOLE, AND ATTACHED TO ITS BASE. IT USES TESSERAE OF VITREOUS GLASS IN VIBRANT COLORS, WHICH WILL NOT FADE WHEN EXPOSED TO THE ELEMENTS.

1 Scale up the template from the back of the book or draw a simple design on brown paper.

2 Make a tracing of the outline of your drawing and cut it out. You will use this later as a template to mark the area of the wall to be covered with cement.

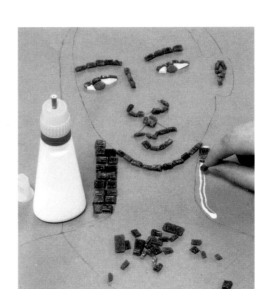

4 Stick these tesserae face down on the main lines of your drawing using water-soluble glue. Stick down any key features, such as the eyes and lips, in contrasting colors. ▶

3 Cut tiles in the outlining color into eighths, using tile nippers.

MATERIALS AND EQUIPMENT YOU WILL NEED

BROWN PAPER • PENCIL • TRACING PAPER • SCISSORS • VITREOUS GLASS MOSAIC TILES, INCLUDING PINK • TILE NIPPERS •
WATER-SOLUBLE GLUE • MIRROR • BOARD • CEMENT-BASED TILE ADHESIVE • MIXING CONTAINER • NOTCHED TROWEL • SPONGE •
SANDPAPER (OPTIONAL) • DILUTED HYDROCHLORIC ACID (OPTIONAL) • GOGGLES (OPTIONAL) • RUBBER GLOVES (OPTIONAL) • SOFT CLOTH

5 Cut pink vitreous glass tiles into quarters. Glue them face down to fill in the areas between the outlines.

6 Cut the mirror into small pieces about the same size as the quartered vitreous glass tesserae.

7 Stick the pieces of mirror face down onto the dress and in the crown.

8 Cut the tiles for the dress and the crown into quarters and glue them face down between the pieces of mirror. Let the paper-backed mosaic dry securely in position.

9 Transfer the mosaic to its final location, carrying it on a board to prevent any tesserae from coming loose. Cut out the tracing paper design and draw around it on the wall or floor. Spread cement-based tile adhesive over this area using a notched trowel, then press the mosaic into it, paper side up. Let dry for about two hours, then dampen the paper with a sponge and gently peel it away. Let dry overnight.

10 Using cement-based tile adhesive, grout the mosaic. Clean off any excess cement with a sponge and let the mosaic dry overnight. Remove any remaining cement with sandpaper. Alternatively, diluted hydrochloric acid can be used, but you must wear goggles and rubber gloves and apply it outside or where there is good ventilation. Wash any acid residue from the surface with plenty of water. Finish by polishing the mosaic with a soft cloth.

CRAZY PAVING CHAIR

THIS CHAIR WAS FOUND REJECTED AND BATTERED IN A JUNK SHOP. WITH A LITTLE WORK AND IMAGINATION, IT HAS BEEN TRANSFORMED INTO AN UNUSUAL, EXCITING PIECE OF FURNITURE. WHILE MOSAIC MAY NOT BE THE FIRST CHOICE FOR COVERING AN OBJECT SUCH AS A CHAIR, THIS EXAMPLE SHOWS THE EXTREMES TO WHICH THE MEDIUM CAN SUCCESSFULLY BE TAKEN. A WHOLE DINING SET DECORATED IN THIS MANNER WOULD BE A MAJOR UNDERTAKING FOR ANY INDIVIDUAL, BUT PARTS OF A CHAIR, SAY THE SEAT OR BACK-REST, COULD BE DECORATED RELATIVELY EASILY. IT IS IMPORTANT TO REALIZE THAT LARGE THREE-DIMENSIONAL OBJECTS SUCH AS THIS CHAIR, WHICH HAS BEEN COVERED WITH TESSERAE CUT FROM A SELECTION OF CHINA, REQUIRE A DECEPTIVELY LARGE AMOUNT OF MOSAIC TO COVER THEM. YOU WOULD BE LUCKY TO FIND ENOUGH OF THE SAME PATTERN TO COVER A WHOLE CHAIR. HERE, THE PROBLEM HAS BEEN SOLVED BY USING SLIGHTLY DIFFERENT PATTERNS OF CHINA TO COVER DIFFERENT SECTIONS OF THE CHAIR.

1 If the chair you have chosen has a padded seat, remove it. There may be a wooden pallet beneath the padding which you can use as a base for the mosaic. If not, cut a piece of plywood to fit in its place.

2 Strip the chair of any paint or varnish and sand down with coarse-grade sandpaper. Then paint the whole chair with diluted white glue.

3 When the surface is dry, stick the seat in place with a strong wood glue and fill any gaps around the edge with cement-based tile adhesive mixed with an admix for extra strength and flexibility.

MATERIALS AND EQUIPMENT YOU WILL NEED
CHAIR • ¾-INCH PLYWOOD (OPTIONAL) • PAINT OR VARNISH STRIPPER • COARSE-GRADE SANDPAPER • PAINTBRUSH •
WHITE GLUE • WOOD GLUE • CEMENT-BASED TILE ADHESIVE • ADMIX FOR TILE ADHESIVE • MIXING CONTAINER • FLEXIBLE KNIFE •
PENCIL OR CHALK • LARGE SELECTION OF CHINA • TILE NIPPERS • RUBBER GLOVES • DILUTED HYDROCHLORIC ACID (OPTIONAL) •
GOGGLES (OPTIONAL) • SOFT CLOTH

4 Draw a design or motifs on any large flat surfaces of the chair with a pencil or chalk. Use simple shapes that are easy to read; this chair will have a large flower on the seat and a heart on the back-rest.

6 Spread cement-based tile adhesive, with admix, within the areas of your design and press the cut china firmly into it.

8 Working on small areas at a time, tile the rest of the chair as in step 6. Where one section of wood meets another, change the pattern of the china you are using.

5 Select china with colors and patterns to suit the motifs you have drawn. Using tile nippers, cut the china into the appropriate shapes and sizes.

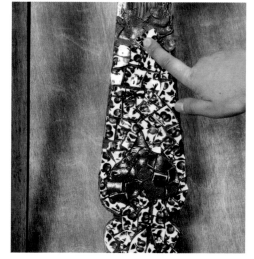

7 Select china to cover the rest of the chair. As you are unlikely to have enough of the same pattern to cover the whole chair, choose two or three patterns that look good together. Cut the china into small, varied shapes.

9 Cut appropriately patterned china into thin slivers and use them to tile the edges of any thin sections of wood. Here, the edges of the back-rest are covered. Let dry for at least 24 hours.

▶

10 Mix up some more cement-based tile adhesive with the admix. Using a flexible knife, smooth this grout into the four corners of every piece of wood. Wearing rubber gloves, rub the grout over the flat surfaces. Work on a small area at a time and try to clean off most of the excess as you go. Let dry overnight.

11 Sand off the excess cement. This can be quite a difficult job, as there are many awkward angles. Alternatively, diluted hydrochloric acid can be used, but you must wear goggles and rubber gloves and apply it outside or where there is good ventilation. Wash any acid residue from the surface with plenty of water and, when dry, polish with a soft cloth.

HOUSE NUMBER PLAQUE

HUNG ON A DOOR FRAME OR FENCE POST, THIS STRIKING NUMBER PLAQUE, DESIGNED BY SARAH ROUND, WILL NOT BE MISSED BY THE MAILMAN. IT IS MADE WITH TESSERAE CUT FROM BRIGHTLY COLORED TILES AND SMALL PIECES OF MIRROR. AS THIS PIECE WILL BE LEFT OUTSIDE ALL YEAR ROUND AND WILL HAVE TO FACE ALL WEATHER CONDITIONS, IT MAY BE A GOOD IDEA TO PAINT THE AREAS OF GROUT WITH A TRANSPARENT WATER SEALANT. IF YOU DO THIS, MAKE SURE YOU CLEAN ANY SEALANT FROM THE SURFACE OF THE TILES. A LARGER PLAQUE COULD BE MADE TO DISPLAY A HOUSE NAME.

1 Cut a piece of ½-inch chipboard to size; the one used here is 7 x 6 inches. Draw the house number on the chipboard, making sure it is at least ⅜ inch wide. If you wish, you can also mark the intended positions of the mirror.

2 Paint the chipboard, front, back and sides, with diluted white glue. Let dry thoroughly.

3 Cut the tiles and mirror into small pieces using tile nippers. First tile the number with the tesserae you have cut, sticking them on the base, one small area at a time, with waterproof tile adhesive. Then tile the area around the number, cutting and applying small pieces of mirror to the marked positions. Wipe off any excess tile adhesive and let the plaque dry for 24 hours.

4 Cover the surface with black outdoor tile grout, making sure all the gaps between the tesserae are well filled, as no moisture must be allowed to penetrate the chipboard base. Spread the grout along the edges of the plaque, then let dry for about ten minutes. Wipe off the excess grout with a sponge and let the plaque dry for 24 more hours. Paint the back of the plaque with an exterior paint and attach a clip for hanging. Finish by polishing the surface of the plaque with a dry, soft cloth and clear glass polish.

MATERIALS AND EQUIPMENT YOU WILL NEED

½-INCH CHIPBOARD • SAW • MARKER • WHITE GLUE • PAINTBRUSHES • TILES IN TWO CONTRASTING COLORS • MIRROR • TILE NIPPERS • WATERPROOF TILE ADHESIVE • MIXING CONTAINER • FLEXIBLE KNIFE • BLACK READY-MIXED OUTDOOR TILE GROUT • GROUT SPREADER • SPONGE • WATERPROOF EXTERIOR PAINT • WALL FASTENING • SCREWS • SCREWDRIVER • SOFT CLOTH • CLEAR GLASS POLISH

MOSAIC PANEL

THIS RICHLY TEXTURED PANEL DESIGNED BY CLEO MUSSI IS COMPOSED OF TESSERAE CUT FROM A VARIETY OF PATTERNED CHINA. MOTIFS ARE CUT OUT AND USED AS FOCAL POINTS FOR THE PATTERNS; SOME ARE RAISED TO GIVE THEM EXTRA EMPHASIS. THESE ARE SURROUNDED AND SEPARATED BY TESSERAE ARRANGED TO FORM STRONG LINEAR ELEMENTS. THE DESIGN HAS BEEN STUCK ONTO A PLYWOOD BASE, RATHER THAN DIRECTLY ONTO THE WALL SURFACE, TO CREATE A MORE THREE-DIMENSIONAL EFFECT. THIS ALSO GIVES THE PANEL THE ADVANTAGE OF BEING PORTABLE.

  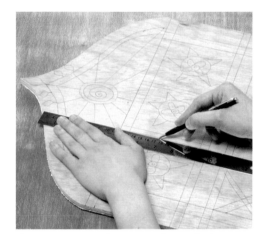

1 Draw the outer shape of the panel onto a sheet of ¾-inch plywood. If you are unsure about drawing directly onto the surface, make a stencil from thick cardboard. Cut out around this shape using a jigsaw and sand down the rough edges. Seal one side and the edges with diluted white glue. Paint the unsealed side (the back) with wood primer, undercoat and then gloss paint, letting each coat dry before applying the next.

2 Mark the position of the mirror plate on the back of the panel. Using the appropriate drill bit, rebate the area that will be under the keyhole-shaped opening, so that it is large enough to take a screw head. Screw the mirror plate in position.

3 Draw your design on the sealed top surface. If necessary, trace and transfer your original design. Tools such as rulers, set squares and compasses are helpful if your design has geometric elements. ▶

MATERIALS AND EQUIPMENT YOU WILL NEED

¾-INCH PLYWOOD • PENCIL • THICK CARDBOARD (OPTIONAL) • JIGSAW • SANDPAPER • WHITE GLUE • PAINTBRUSHES • WOOD PRIMER • WHITE UNDERCOAT • GLOSS PAINT • MIRROR PLATE • DRILL AND REBATE BIT • ¾-INCH SCREWS • SCREWDRIVER • TRACING PAPER (OPTIONAL) • RULER, SET SQUARE OR COMPASS (OPTIONAL) • SELECTION OF CHINA • TILE NIPPERS • TILE ADHESIVE • POWDERED TILE GROUT • MIXING CONTAINER • CEMENT DYE, VINYL MATTE LATEX OR ACRYLIC PAINT (OPTIONAL) • RUBBER GLOVES • SQUEEGEE OR FLEXIBLE KNIFE • NAILBRUSH • SOFT CLOTH

4 Sort the china into groups according to color and pattern and select interesting motifs that could be used to form the centerpieces of designs. Using the tile nippers, cut the china into the desired shapes.

5 Using smooth edges cut from cups and plates and ready-mixed tile adhesive, tile the edges of the panel. Then use small, regular-shaped tesserae to tile the structural lines of the design. Press the pieces in the adhesive first.

6 Raise small areas of the mosaic to give greater emphasis to sections of the design by setting the tesserae on a larger mound of tile adhesive. Cut more china and use it to form the patterns between the structural lines. Let the panel dry for 24 hours.

7 Mix powdered grout with water. If you wish the grout to have a color, add cement dye, vinyl matte latex or acrylic paint to the mixture (if this is to be used indoors, cement dye is not essential). Wearing rubber gloves, spread the grout over the surface using a squeegee or a flexible knife. Rub the grout into the gaps with your fingers.

8 Let the surface dry for a few minutes, then scrub off any excess grout using a stiff nailbrush.

9 Let dry for 24 hours, then polish the surface with a soft cloth.

TEMPLATES

PRINCESS WALL MOSAIC PP. 79–81

BATHROOM CABINET PP. 46–47

SPLASHBACK PP. 48–51

SUPPLIERS

The majority of the materials needed to make these mosaic projects can be found at most do-it-yourself or hardware stores. Most large tile stores will order specialty mosaic materials for you if they do not have them in stock. Listed below are some of the better known specialty suppliers as well as more general suppliers that may be of use when making the projects illustrated in this book.

Alice's Stained Glass
7015 N. 58th Ave.
Glendale, AZ 85301
Tel: (602) 939-7260

The Art Store
935 Erie Blvd. E.
Syracuse, NY 13210
Tel: (315) 474-1000

Brian's Crafts Unlimited
1421 S. Dixie Freeway
New Smyrna Beach, FL 32168
Tel: (904) 672-2726

Bryne Ceramics
95 Bartley Road
Flanders, NJ 07836
Tel: (201) 584-7492

Covington Engineering Corp.
715 W. Colton Ave.
P.O. Box 35
Redlands, CA 92374
Tel: (909) 793-6636

Creative Craft House
897 San Jose Circle, HC 62
P.O. Box 7810
Bullhead City, AZ 86430
Tel: (520) 754-3300

Denver Glass Machinery, Inc.
3065 S. Umatilla St.
Englewood, CO 80110
Tel: (303) 781-0980

Dick Blick
P.O. Box 1267
Galesburg, IL 61402
Tel: (309) 343-6181

Eastern Art Glass
P.O. Box 341
Wyckoff, NJ 07481
Tel: (201) 847-0001

Glass Craft, Inc.
626 Moss St.
Golden, CO 80401
Tel: (303) 278-4670

Hudson Glass Co., Inc.
219 N. Division St.
Peekskill, NY 10566
Tel: (914) 737-2124

Minnesota/Midwest Clay.
8001 Grand Ave. S.
Bloomington, MN 55420
Tel: (612) 884-9101,
(800) 252-9872

ACKNOWLEDGMENTS

The author would like to thank Bill and Theresa Baird for all their help during the course of writing this book.

The author and publishers would also like to thank the following for their contributions: Tessa Brown, Sandra Hadfield, Cleo Mussi, Sarah Round and Norma Vondee

Thanks also to Gideon at Upstart Gallery, and all the mosaicists who kindly lent their pieces for photography.

INDEX